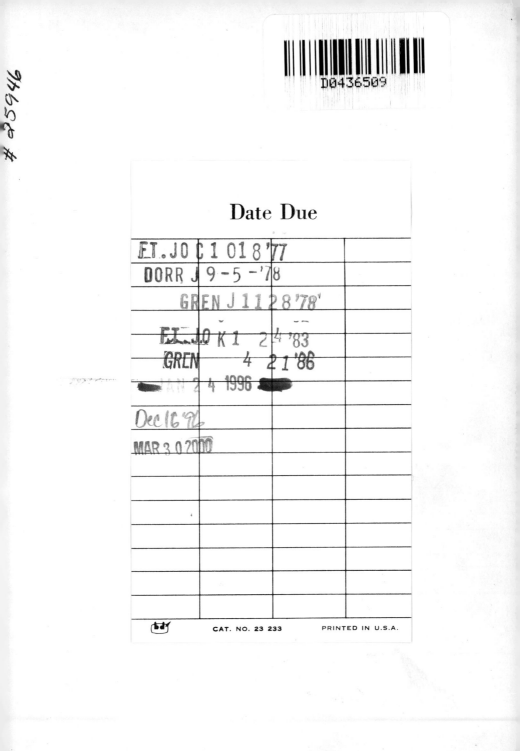

## Date Due

| | | |
|---|---|---|
| FT.JO C1 01 8 '77 | | |
| DORR J 9-5 -'78 | | |
| GREN J 11 2 8 '78' | | |
| FT.JO K1 2 4 '83 | | |
| GREN 4 2 1 '86 | | |
| JAN 2 4 1996 | | |
| Dec 16 '96 | | |
| MAR 3 0 2000 | | |
| | | |
| | | |
| | | |
| | | |
| | | |
| | | |

*the true story of*

# ALBERT EINSTEIN

## MAN OF SCIENCE

### BY RUTH L. OLDFIELD

## CHILDRENS PRESS, CHICAGO

# Author and Artist

Ruth L. Oldfield decided when she was a young girl that she would be an engineer, and at twenty became the first girl to graduate from the electronics engineering course at RCA Institutes. After two years as an engineer in a research and development laboratory, she switched to technical publications. She has been writing happily about science and engineering ever since. Her previous work includes *Radio-Television and Basic Electronics, The Practical Dictionary of Electricity and Electronics, Theory and Application of Silicon Solar Cells,* and many technical manuals. Mrs. Oldfield is Course Supervisor, Communications Courses, Britannica Schools and executive editor of *Astron,* the monthly publication of the Chicago Section of the Institute of Electrical and Electronics Engineers. She lives in Chicago with her physicist husband and her two children, Elizabeth and Fred. Elizabeth read this book in manuscript and made certain suggestions, some of which her mother agreed with.

Parviz Sadighian was born in Tehran, Iran, in 1939. He was graduated from the Academy of Fine Arts in Tehran and received a partial scholarship for foreign study. In 1959 he enrolled at the Art Institute in Chicago and continued his studies in sculpture and in painting. Interest in painting led to courses in illustration and advertising art. Mr. Sadighian is now associated with the Bert Ray Studio in Chicago.

Library of Congress Catalog Card Number: 64-19880
Copyright © 1964 by Childrens Press
Lithographed in the U.S.A.

# Contents

# *Foreword*

Stories were told about Albert Einstein even while he was still alive. Many of these were based on true happenings, but many were not. He was amused by many of the stories and never attempted to correct a wrong impression. He himself considered only a few events in his early life important enough to write down, and then only sketchily. He put almost no personal details in the only autobiography he wrote, stating: "For the essential in the being of a man of my type lies precisely in *what* he thinks and *how* he thinks, not in what he does or suffers." So the stories became legends, and Albert Einstein did not feel it was necessary to correct them.

In writing a book about his life, therefore, a conscientious biographer is faced with the problem: "Did this or that incident really take place? Did it take place, but were the reasons for the incident different from those frequently given?" Certain facts are easy to authenticate. He was born in Ulm, Germany, on March 14, 1879. His parents moved to Munich the year after he was born. He was married twice and had two sons by his first wife. He died April 18, 1955.

But what of all the facts beyond these? What sort of a *person* was he? What were his friends like? Did he play the violin like a virtuoso or was he merely a talented amateur? What were his sons named? What sort of a father was he? The list is almost endless.

A number of good biographies of Einstein have been written for adults. Incidents and traits described in some are described differently, or omitted, in others. Before writing this biography, therefore, I read much of what Albert Einstein wrote about himself; about his scientific ideas; and about his ideas on peace and war, and many humanitarian causes. As I read, one thing became clear: here was a man who not only set down the ideas on which modern physics is based, but also was concerned with humanity. This much I could glean from his own writings, and whenever possible I have used his words to illustrate his principles. The personal details about his life I obtained from those biographies which seemed most complete. *Einstein On Peace,* edited by Otto Nathan and Heinz Norden, was particularly valuable, for all of Einstein's writings on peace and humanitarian causes are collected in it. In addition, the editors have provided a background for each piece so that the book helps the reader to picture clearly Germany in the 1920's, the United States in the 1930's, etc. Assessment of Einstein's influence on science, as well as Einstein's own "Autobiographical Notes," appear in *Albert Einstein: Philosopher-Scientist,* edited by Paul Arthur Schilpp.

A work of this sort always reflects the author as well as the subject. I have tried to answer the questions asked in the previous paragraphs as fully as I could. The publisher and I both hope that the reader will see a true picture of Albert Einstein reflected in this work.

Ruth L. Oldfield

Chicago, Ill.
June, 1964

Out yonder there was this huge world, which exists independently of us human beings and which stands before us like a great, eternal riddle, at least partially accessible to our inspection and thinking.

Albert Einstein, "Autobiographical Notes"

# A Wonder of Nature

A snowy evening in Munich, January 1883; a boy of four peers out the window of the parlor, trying to see through the whirling flakes. The gas lamp outside the front door casts a feeble glow through the gloom. At last the child hears the sounds he has been waiting for; a horse and carriage drive up to the house.

"It's Papa, it's Papa!" shouts young Albert Einstein, running to the door. The door opens and Hermann Einstein enters, carrying cold and snow with him. The delighted boy rushes to him, is picked up, hugged, then thrown in the air.

Pauline Einstein appears suddenly in the hall. "Albert— Albert, let your Papa take his coat off. Dinner is ready. And look, your hands are dirty again."

The father laughs. "Go with your Mama and wash your hands, my son. Who knows, after we eat I may even have something for you."

Albert goes willingly enough but is so excited about the "something" that he cannot eat until his mother tells him, "It is all very well for you to want what your Papa has for you, but you do not get anything until you have eaten your dinner every mouthful."

Albert manages to choke down his dinner, but he doesn't think Papa will ever finish; and *then* Papa lights his after-dinner cigar. The boy tries to be patient, but squirms in his chair—stopping abruptly when his mother shakes her head at him. Finally his father smiles at him.

"Well, Albert. Were you a good boy today?"

"Oh, yes, Papa. At least—" his face clouds up for a moment "—at least most of the time. Mama scolded me twice," he is forced to confess.

"For a boy who was scolded only twice, perhaps I *do* have something."

Hermann Einstein makes a great show of searching through all his pockets. "Now where can that package be?" he asks. "I was sure I had put it in that one." Finally, with Albert feeling he can stand it not one minute longer, he pulls a small package out of his inner pocket.

Albert opens it eagerly. It is a small round case, covered with glass and containing a needle balanced on a pin. Albert does not see why this is such a special thing. It is not a puzzle—there is no other place to put the needle; he turns it over, but the metal case is unmarked. Perhaps it makes a noise? He raises his arm to shake it, but his father stops him.

"Gently, gently, my boy. You'll ruin it that way."

"But Papa, what is it?"

"A compass."

"A compass," Albert echoes, looking at it. At least this mysterious something has a name. "But what does it do?"

His father laughs. "See how the needle is black at one end?

That end always points to the north. Look, no matter how you turn the compass, the black end of the needle always swings around so it points to the north."

"The black end always turns to the north?" Albert asks. Here is a mystery indeed—much too much for a tired excited boy of four to take in all at once. "But why does it? Does the color make it turn north? Why not the other end of the needle?"

"No, the color is there only so you will know which end of the needle to look at. The needle is a magnet, and the earth has a big magnet in the north. The needle swings around because it is attracted to the magnet in the earth."

The boy looks at the compass with new respect. It always swings to the north—and it is a magnet! So much for a little needle to be and do. Could it really always work? "I will try it," he announces and hurries from the room. He knows the kitchen window faces east—the early morning sun comes through it. He rushes to the kitchen, facing the window. The needle in the compass is swinging wildly, but as he watches, it slows down and stops. And the black end points not toward the east, but to his left—toward the north! Here is a wonder indeed! But will it work every time? Every single time? He rushes from room to room, always facing in a different direction. Each time the needle swings, then stops pointing north. It works! Every single time!

"Papa, Papa," Albert shouts rushing back to show him. "It works, it really works, every single time."

His parents laugh at his earnestness.

"Yes, Albert, it works every single time," his father agrees. "And this summer when we go to the mountains you can take it along; then you will always know which direction is north, so you won't get lost."

"And I'll show Elsa how it works."

"When it's time for the mountains, you can show Elsa," his mother says. "But now it is time for a boy to go to bed, so he can rest and grow. And in the summer when we see Elsa, you can show her. But now you must put away the compass and get ready for bed."

The boy goes to his room with his mother. He can hardly bear to put the compass down, but his mother finally persuades him and he lays it slowly on his bedside table. He keeps glancing at it while getting ready for bed.

Just think of it: such a little needle and it always turns to the north. Why should this be? Why should this magnet—and just what is a magnet?—why should this magnet do this? He lies awake in the dark wondering about this. It is the first time the little boy has ever known this sense of wonder. He is not aware at the time what a profound impression this makes on him.

But sixty-three years later, writing what he himself called his "obituary," he remembers: "That this needle behaved in such a determined way did not at all fit into the nature of events, which could find a place in the unconscious world of concepts (effect connected with direct 'touch'). I can still remember—or at least believe I remember—that this experience made a deep and lasting impression upon me. Something deeply hidden had to be behind things. What man sees before him from infancy causes no reaction of this kind; he is not surprised over the falling of bodies, concerning wind and rain, nor concerning the moon or about the fact that the moon does not fall down, nor concerning the differences between living and non-living matter."

Spring came slowly that year, then summer. The family went to the mountains as always, and Albert showed off his compass to his cousin Elsa.

Another year passed. Albert approached school age. His family were Jewish, although like many German Jews of that time they had lost most of the traditional Jewish customs and rituals. They thought of themselves as Germans, primarily, who were of Jewish descent. All the schools in Munich at that time were parochial schools. A child went to a Jewish school if he was Jewish; he went to a Roman Catholic school if he was Roman Catholic; he went to a Protestant school if he was Protestant. Munich was primarily a Catholic city, with relatively few Jewish families. So there were many Roman Catholic parochial schools, but relatively few Jewish schools. And the closest Jewish school was halfway across the city. Frau Einstein worried about the traveling that Albert would have to do. She was determined that Albert go to a closer school. After all, they were not such pious Jews—could Albert be hurt by going to the nearby Roman Catholic school? Like a good German wife, she suggested this to her husband.

"Hermann," she began one evening after the children were in bed. "I am worried about Albert."

Hermann Einstein looked up from his book in astonishment. "About Albert? He seemed perfectly all right this evening."

Frau Einstein sighed. Hermann was being difficult, and that made it harder for her. "This evening. Yes, well, this evening of course he was all right. It is when he starts to school that I worry about."

Her husband laughed. "Now, Pauline, you are borrowing trouble again. He is a quiet child and often likes to play by himself, but he will be all right in school. I am sure he will learn once he starts to school. Most children do."

"Of course, he will learn! He is quiet only because he thinks so much. Some day he will probably be a professor. But that is not what I am worried about. It is the long way he will have to go to school. If he goes to the Jewish school, that is."

"If he goes to the Jewish school," Hermann echoed his wife. "What do you mean? Of course he goes to the Jewish school."

"The Catholic school is much closer. Perhaps he could go there."

"Go there?" Herr Einstein was startled. The volume of Schiller he had been reading dropped unnoticed to the floor. "But Pauline, we are Jewish. How would Albert feel in a Catholic school? And would they even accept him? They have their own children to teach."

"You could at least talk to the brother in charge of the school. We are not such observing Jews that Albert would be unhappy. Please, Hermann. He is still so little and the Jewish school is so far."

14

"But, Pauline," Hermann Einstein protested. Frau Einstein frowned and he could see that she was determined about this. He sighed. "Very well, I will talk to him. But don't be disappointed if he won't admit Albert."

Frau Einstein smiled. "I am sure he will take our Albert. Will you talk to him tomorrow?"

"Tomorrow. Now are you satisfied?"

Frau Einstein picked up the sweater she was knitting for Albert. "Thank you, Hermann. I am sure he will do well in school."

True to his promise, Herr Einstein spoke to the head of the school the next day, explaining the problem. It was finally agreed that young Albert could attend the Catholic school, although he would have to attend the religion classes with the rest of the students. Since the Einsteins were non-observing Jews (that is, they did not follow the traditional customs and rituals of Judaism), this did not particularly bother them.

So Albert started to school. True to his father's prediction, he did learn, although slowly. He was not very popular with his classmates, for he was not much interested in games or in playing soldier. He preferred being by himself, thinking or dreaming. His thoughts were not of his school work, however, and his teachers were continually after him to pay attention. Finally, the teachers decided he was retarded and sent a report to his father, stating that young Albert was "mentally slow, unsociable, and adrift forever in his foolish dreams."

Yet when the boy's interest was aroused in something, he worked hard at it. Although he did not play much with his schoolmates, he would "lecture" to them on the subjects he was interested in. These subjects, however, rarely interested the other boys; as a result he was nicknamed *Pater Langweil,* Father Bore.

Although Albert did not do particularly well in school, these were still happy years for him. The atmosphere at home was warm and loving. His mother was a talented pianist and she played often, usually the compositions of Beethoven, which she loved. She insisted that Albert study music, and at six he started to study the violin. Although he enjoyed playing the violin, he enjoyed practicing no more than any other young boy.

Albert's father was not particularly musical. He did, however, enjoy reading the great works of German literature. Albert grew up in a household where Goethe and Schiller were familiar names.

Because Albert had to attend classes in religion at the Catholic school, he became much interested in religious thought. He felt for several years that religion alone offered a meaning to life beyond that of merely existing. To the surprise and consternation of his parents, he became very religious. This religious feeling added to his strong feeling for always telling the truth. His classmates often made fun of him because of this insistence on telling the truth at all times.

At ten, Albert Einstein entered Luitpold Gymnasium in

Munich. (A gymnasium, pronounced ghim · NAH · zee · um, is similar to high school in this country.) The teachers were even less sympathetic and kind than those at the lower school had been. Discipline was rigid; pupils were forced to stand erect when they wished to answer a question put by a teacher. Questions from the pupils were discouraged. The students were there to learn facts, not to question why the facts were so.

The insistence on rote learning, as well as the rigid discipline, repelled Albert Einstein. At home, he had always been encouraged to ask questions. Being skeptical by nature, he often questioned the philosophy of the subjects taught, as well as the facts. None of the masters were used to this type of student, and they disapproved. The more outside reading Einstein did, particularly in the fields of science and mathematics, the more questions he raised in class. The more he questioned, the more the masters disciplined him. He retaliated by likening his teachers to the sergeants and lieutenants in the German Army—a particularly ignorant, vulgar, and cruel group.

The gymnasium left Einstein with a strong dislike for rigid academic training, requirements, and philosophy. Even toward the end of his life, he still felt bitter about this type of training. When a young college physics major asked Einstein how best to study physics, Einstein replied that the young man must learn all he could from his textbooks. "Read them over and over," he urged, "until you master them." The teachers, Einstein felt, would stifle any originality or talent the student had. Einstein's views on orthodox training in science were undoubtedly shaped by his unique gifts as well as by his school experiences. He perhaps did not realize that although his advice is good for that unique person the world will later hail as a "genius," the rest of us are less able to "go it alone." We need the aid and advice of experienced teachers. Fortunately, teachers and their ways of teaching have changed radically since Einstein's young days.

The years between ten and thirteen were crucial ones for young Einstein. He made three discoveries that foreshadowed his life. He discovered the music of Mozart; he discovered mathematics; and he discovered science.

Although he had studied the violin from the age of six, he had never cared for practicing—a sign that even a genius is not too different from other little boys. But then his teacher gave him his first long Mozart piece. He was overjoyed. To think that there was music for the violin that sounded like that! Such melody, such clarity, such purity of tone. Albert rushed home and started to play—and found that years of "skimping" on his practice time showed up immediately. He could not play the Mozart properly. There were the notes on the page; he could hear the music as his teacher had played it. But it did not sound that way when he attempted it. He began to practice in earnest, devoting hours to the scales and tricky bowing practice he had previously hated. As he had been told, practicing made the difference. His technique improved and he was able to play the Mozart piece, the first of many he was to play. From then on, no matter how busy, he always found time to practice. Music, indeed, became for

18

him a way of working out problems. Whenever he was tired or dispirited, he turned to his violin. He was to find music a solace in many grim hours that he could not even dream of at ten. And everywhere he went he made friends of musicians as well as physicists, for he spoke the language of the musician as he spoke that of the physicist.

Hermann Einstein's brother Jacob was his partner in the small electrochemical factory. He had trained as an engineer and was delighted when his young nephew asked searching questions. Jacob showed the boy how to work algebra problems. "Pretend that this symbol we call $x$ is a wild animal. But you don't know which wild animal. Hunt it down by doing the problem. Once you have solved the problem, you have found the identity of the animal." Albert became a fierce "hunter," soon able to identify the "animal" no matter how tangled the trail.

When Albert was about twelve, his school subjects included geometry. He was given a copy of Euclid's geometry before the beginning of the school year. The book fascinated him. He worked through all the proofs before the class had started. Once again he was swept by a sense of awe and wonder that things such as these actually existed. In his autobiography he recalled how the lucidity and certainty of the proofs impressed him. Here was his second great wonder: "that man is capable at all to reach such a degree of certainty and purity in pure thinking as the Greeks showed us for the first time to be possible in geometry."

At about this time Max Talmey, a young Russian medical

student, began to come to the Einstein house for dinner every Thursday evening. Max enjoyed talking to Albert and Albert looked forward to Thursday evenings. Here was someone who knew about another aspect of the world of nature. Albert questioned Max so extensively that Pauline Einstein felt she had to interfere.

"Albert, leave Max alone. He comes for dinner, not to tutor you. How can you be so rude to a guest?"

"But I was not being rude, Mama. I was only asking Max..."

"Enough, Albert," his father interrupted. "You bother Max so he cannot eat in peace. And sometimes your mother and I also would like to talk to our guest."

Max laughed. "Albert doesn't really bother me, Herr Einstein. I like talking to him."

"Nevertheless," Hermann Einstein insisted, "Albert must learn to let others talk also."

The following Thursday Max was a bit late. The family was almost ready to sit down to supper when he appeared. As Albert began to tell Max what he had been doing, his mother intervened.

"Remember what we spoke about last week, Albert?"

"Don't worry, Frau Einstein," Max said. "I have finally solved the problem of how to satisfy Albert's curiosity and still have time to talk to you and Herr Einstein."

After supper, Max handed Albert a package. Albert tore open the wrappings. "*The People's Book on Natural Science, Volume I*," he read the title in a subdued voice. "By Aaron

Bernstein. Oh, Max. Thank you, thank you."

"I could only afford to get him the first volume" Max Talmey was saying apologetically to Herr Einstein. I think he is very talented. Perhaps you could, yourself. . . ."

"My dear Talmey, of course. How splendid of you to have even thought of doing this for him."

"Max, do you really think our Albert is talented?" asked Frau Einstein. "You are not saying this just because you are fond of him?"

"No, indeed. I think he is very talented—perhaps even exceptionally talented. Haven't you noticed how he takes nothing for granted, and questions everything? And then he can tell you more about what you thought you were telling him than you know."

"But why does he not get along in school? They are always complaining about his behavior."

"Just because he asks such questions. You know yourself that this is not encouraged in the gymnasium. Even in medical school . . ." his voice trailed off and he sighed.

The Bernstein volumes showed Albert tantalizing glimpses of the various fields of natural science. Plants; animals; the interdependence of plants, animals, and man; the heavenly universe; the geology of the earth—all were covered in a popularly written style. Albert read through all the volumes almost without stopping. He reread and reread them. Explanations such as these merely whetted his appetite for stronger dishes. He went on to read other books, particularly books that attempted to organize all the scientific knowledge of the time into a single scheme. Such a naturalistic viewpoint of the universe rejected religious interpretations of the universe. Albert soon came to believe that many of the stories in the Bible were not true. He knew that the accounts of nature that he was reading now did not agree with the Biblical accounts.

His natural skepticism reasserted itself. Was this another one of the "lies" that a harsh, authoritarian state was insisting on? His preoccupation with religion ended as abruptly as it had begun. In addition, Albert became even more skeptical and suspicious toward authority than he had been previously.

The books on science that Albert read and his conversations with Max Talmey showed him that anyone interested in physical science must know mathematics. He went on studying at home, mastering the principles of differential and integral calculus. He became more and more impatient with the problems assigned to the mathematics classes, and frequently allowed his irritation to show.

By the time Albert was about fifteen Max Talmey had completed his medical training in Munich and had emigrated to New York. The Einstein factory had been losing money, and Hermann Einstein finally decided to give it up. The Einsteins decided to leave Munich and go to Milan, Italy, where a branch of the family was already established. But there was Albert and his schooling to consider. Hermann Einstein was a conscientious father and wanted to see Albert go on in one of the professions. Even at that time, a college education was necessary training for the professions. And to enter a European university a boy had to have a certificate from a gymnasium. So the matter was settled in Hermann Einstein's mind before it even came up. Albert must stay in Munich and finish his gymnasium work. Herr Einstein found a family Albert could board with.

His sister, Maja, of course, went with their parents. A girl did not expect a university education in those days. She could learn the art of keeping house by helping her mother. Albert watched his family off, then went back to his room. It seemed even bleaker now that he was alone than it had when he had moved his books in with his father's help. Even the bright cushions that Maja had made for his bed did not help his mood any. In depression, he turned to his books and was even less sociable with his schoolmates than before.

Maja wrote often, long letters giving Albert news of the entire family. Albert grew more and more lonely. His health reflected this and he had many severe colds. He finally thought of a way he could join his family in Italy. Max Talmey's brother was a physician in Munich. Albert persuaded him to certify that Albert must leave school to regain his health.

Albert next went to his mathematics instructor. Could the instructor give him a letter stating that Einstein had enough mathematics so he could enter a university to study higher mathematics? His teacher certainly could. One even suspects that the teacher was relieved at the thought of no longer having to lecture to a class in which one of the students knew more than he.

Before Albert could turn his medical certificate in to the gymnasium, however, he was summoned to the headmaster's office.

"Einstein, you will have to leave," the headmaster informed him.

"But why? What have I done?"

"Your teachers complain of your attitude. Your presence destroys the respect of the rest of the class for their teachers. You are always questioning the teacher in a disrespectful manner."

"I don't mean to be disrespectful. But when someone says something that seems stupid, I . . ."

"Enough. That is just what your teachers complain of. Your very presence in class destroys the respect of the other students. How long could the gymnasium continue if all students thought as you do?"

Albert could not answer that, although he wondered if it would really be such a loss if the gymnasium did not continue. If that was the attitude of the teachers toward a student who wanted to know why facts were true, perhaps it might be better if the gymnasium did not continue. He was wise enough, however, to keep this idea to himself.

So Albert Einstein left Germany and joined his family in Milan. For six months or so he did no work. He and Maja took long walking trips, stopping at noon to eat a picnic lunch. They visited museums and cathedrals. And the music! Everywhere Albert went there was music. Even the peasants sang. The music in the concert halls and at La Scala was more beautiful than any Albert had ever heard before.

Once again, Hermann Einstein's business failed. He was forced to move the family to Pavia. And here the Einsteins had to face the fact that they would probably never regain the money and position they had had when the children were born. Hermann Einstein worried about his son, who appeared to be enjoying his stay in Italy with little thought about the future. Another family conference was called.

"Albert, you know business is not good for us just now. I can't support you any longer. You will have to support yourself. Have you thought of becoming an electrical engineer?"

Albert shook his head. "Engineering does not appeal to me. Only to make things work—no, I want to know why they work. If I study mathematics and physics perhaps I can learn something."

His father was shocked. "Learn something!" he shouted. "I am talking about earning a living and you start talking philosophy. It is time to forget this philosophical nonsense and concentrate on learning a sensible trade like electrical engineering. Then your mother and I can be proud of you."

"No," Albert said stubbornly. "That I cannot do. I want to study physics—perhaps some day I will do something even in physics that you and Mama can be proud of."

No amount of argument could shake Albert. Physics, he knew, was right for him. It was only a question of where to study. At last his father agreed. Albert would go to Zurich, Switzerland, and enter the Swiss Federal Polytechnic School, one of the foremost schools in Europe.

In a man of my type the turning-point of the development lies in the fact that gradually the major interest disengages itself from the momentary and the merely personal and turns towards the striving for a mental grasp of things.

Albert Einstein, "Autobiographical Notes"

# The Young Einstein

The family all came to see Albert off for Zurich. They were pleased that Albert was going, yet already lonely for him. Even Maja was not chattering as much as usual. His mother wiped her eyes furtively as he said his goodbys. There seemed little chance that she would see him until he finished his education, and even then—well, who could tell how things would turn out?

A few days after leaving his family in Italy, Albert took the entrance examinations for the Zurich Polytechnic School. The mathematics examination was a snap; the physical sciences, also. When he came to the biological sciences, he could only stare at the paper in dismay. All that time when he had been studying mathematics, other students had been cramming in facts in botany and zoology. Now they were happily writing examination papers, while he . . . Albert sighed and decided he would do his best. But worse was yet to come. The school actually expected him to have some proficiency in modern languages. German, of course, was his mother tongue, but French was also required. He wrote the paper, aware that his preparation had been woefully inadequate for this type of examination.

He did not go back to the school until the results of the examinations were posted. The hall in front of the bulletin board was crowded with candidates reading the names of those who had been admitted. Einstein searched the list carefully. His name was not on it. His knowledge of mathematics and physics had not been enough to gain him entrance! As he was turning away, he caught sight of a small notice stating: The Director will see the following candidates in his office. There, finally, was his name. Could there be hope he might yet be admitted? Einstein rushed off to the Director's office.

"Ah, yes, Einstein," the Director greeted him. "You have an extraordinary knowledge of mathematics for a candidate. Too bad your knowledge in other subjects is not as good."

"Then there is no hope that I can be admitted?"

"No hope? There is always hope; however, you will have to make up the work you do not have."

"Make it up? But how? What books do you recommend? I can study mathematics on my own, but I don't know that I can study French that way."

The Director laughed. "I am not suggesting that you study on your own. Go back to school; complete your work and earn a certificate. Then we can admit you."

"Back to school?" Albert was dumfounded at the suggestion. "Back to Munich? I never could learn anything at that school."

"I dare say. No, I meant here in Switzerland. I would suggest the cantonal school at Aarau. I think you will like both the town and the school, and I know that the teachers are good."

"Very well, sir. If you recommend the school, I will try it."

"Good. We will look forward to seeing you back here next year then, Einstein."

The small town of Aarau was a friendly one. The school was far different from the ones Albert had known in Germany. Students were actually expected and encouraged to think! The physics and chemistry classrooms had apparatus for demonstrating physical principles! The students were expected to *use* the apparatus in the physics laboratory, not to sit quietly watching an instructor demonstrate some physical principle. Using a microscope in the zoology and botany courses made Albert feel that the time was not being altogether lost. He was seeing below the surface, even if just below, at least in those courses. Since the teachers encouraged the kind of independent work and skepticism he had always had, he felt at ease for the first time in a formal school atmosphere.

One of the teachers at the school so enjoyed having Albert as a student that he invited him to stay with his own family. The warm, friendly family welcomed Albert. Mrs. Winteler worried because Albert was so thin and made special dishes to tempt his appetite. Professor Winteler spent long hours discussing naturalism and religion with Albert. Best of all, Karl Winteler, just Albert's age, studied with him, argued with him, played music with him. At last Albert had a friend his own age with similar interests. Albert and Karl and Karl's sister often hiked into the mountains surrounding Aarau, sometimes heading toward Zurich, sometimes toward Luzern (Lucerne) about forty kilometers (twenty-five miles) away. They often followed the Suhr River to Sursee, twenty-eight kilometers (eighteen miles) away on a small lake called Sempacher See.

The year at Aarau was over sooner than Einstein had expected. He went back to Zurich with a certificate from the cantonal school and was admitted to the Polytechnic School, in the education department. He had decided while at Aarau that as a teacher he could support himself, yet still have time to do the original research he felt he must do.

The last two decades of the nineteenth century were a time of much ferment in physics. James Clerk Maxwell had proposed his electromagnetic theory. Heinrich Hertz had discovered the photoelectric effect. Albert A. Michelson and Edward W. Morley had measured the speed of light and had found no effect of the motion of the earth through the ether. The young Einstein read the reports of these discoveries. Even at seventeen it seemed evident to him that classical physics based on the mechanics of Newton could not explain the new observations. Although it was evident to Einstein, it was not evident to most of the older physicists. One of the exceptions was Ernst Mach, the great Austrian physicist. Mach analyzed Newtonian mechanics in his book, *History of Mechanics,* and showed that the principles of this mechanics are not self-evident. Einstein was greatly influenced by this work. He felt that he could find some of the great underlying principles of physics if he left Newtonian mechanics behind. But to be able to do this, he first had to, know more mathematics and, particularly, more physics. He plunged into his work at the Polytechnic School with much eagerness.

During these years Einstein met Mileva Maric, a young Serbian girl whose family lived in southeastern Hungary. Like Einstein, she had always been the odd one in her class—a girl who insisted on studying physics! She had no intention of marrying and indeed was rather hostile to Einstein when he began to talk to her. But he ignored this and they began to go walking together, talking over the work they had been doing in the physics laboratory.

Albert and Mileva were frequently joined by Friedrich Adler, a young Austrian. He had been sent to Zurich by his father, Viktor Adler, in the hopes that he would stay out of politics. Interested as Friedrich was in physics, he was still interested in politics. He would never become a Social Democrat politician like his father, but social injustice "burned him up." When he came along, talks were as likely to develop along political lines as along physical ones.

Albert had kept his interest in music and still practiced whenever he could. Occasionally he and Mileva managed to scrape together enough money for tickets to a concert or a recital. Both of them were living on very small allowances from home. Mileva's family could afford very little and Einstein was receiving an allowance of one hundred Swiss francs (about twenty-five dollars) from relatives in Italy. He had been stateless since he had renounced his German citizenship;

now he was determined to become a Swiss citizen. Out of the hundred francs, he saved twenty every month so he could have the necessary fee when he applied for his citizenship papers. Einstein realized that Swiss citizenship would probably be necessary before he could be appointed to a good job in one of the Swiss universities. He had been happier in Switzerland than ever before. He would express his appreciation by becoming a citizen. The lack of money, however, did not disturb Albert as much as it might have at one of our American colleges. Many of the things he enjoyed most were free, and most of his friends had very little money.

He did, however, manage to scrape up enough each year to go to Italy during the long vacations to see his family. Maja had grown into a charming woman who was now interested in studying philosophy. The family still had little money as Hermann Einstein's business kept getting worse instead of better. Perhaps, thought Albert, when I am through with my training I can manage to send Maja a little something each month. His parents were always delighted to see him, but Albert noticed sadly that they seemed considerably older at each visit. In 1900, while Albert was in Switzerland, his father died. Now Albert was the man in the Einstein family.

He took his final examinations at the Polytechnic School and did brilliantly. Now he would surely be offered a good position and he could contribute to the support of his mother and sister. And there was Mileva. She, too, had finished her schooling in 1900 and would have to look for a position. Albert decided that he knew just the position for her.

"Mileva," he teased. "Have you given any thought to your future? What are you going to do now that you have passed your examinations?"

"Do? Albert, are you crazy? You know what I am going to do. I shall get a job as a teaching assistant, perhaps even here, and go on with my physics."

"I was thinking of offering you a position as my wife."

"Oh, Albert," Mileva said softly, "you know how fond I am of you. Fonder than I had thought I could be of anyone. And for you to ask me to be your wife!" She paused for a few minutes. "But I don't see how I can. I have dreamed of being a physicist since I was a little girl. I can't give it up now."

"Perhaps you could combine being a physicist and a wife," Albert suggested. "Madame Curie does so—and she seems to be a competent physicist."

Mileva considered this in silence for a few minutes. The news that Madame Curie and her husband had discovered a new element had electrified the physics students two years earlier. "But I am afraid I am not Madame Curie, nor are you her husband. I do not think either of us would be happy that way. No, either I am a physicist or I am your wife."

"So you will not consider this?"

"Let me be a physicist first Albert. After we have both worked for a while, perhaps I will feel differently." And with that Albert Einstein had to be content.

In the meantime, there was the practical matter of finding jobs. Albert was certain he would have no problems here.

He had graduated with honors in mathematics and physics and his professors had praised him as one of the most talented students ever to graduate from Zurich. Albert decided to apply for a job as what would be called a "teaching assistant" in an American university. He would teach and do some original research under the guidance of an experienced professor.

Albert went to the physics professor he most respected and asked about such an assistantship.

"Einstein," he stammered, "I-I had no idea you would be interested. If you had said something sooner. The fact is— I have already someone for next year." He mentioned a man who was competent but not brilliant. "I am sure you will find something. Try one of the other professors."

Albert did. The answer was always the same, nothing available. Each professor assured Albert he had a brilliant future, but he, personally could offer no job. Albert couldn't understand it.

"What's wrong with me?" he burst out suddenly one day as he was being refused a job. "Why do you tell me how brilliant I am and then refuse to let me work with you? How can I ever tell whether I am brilliant if I never get started?"

The professor turned red with shame. "Albert, we are not talking here of your ability. But it takes more in life than ability. People must like you, and . . ."

". . . And they don't? What have I done?"

"It is nothing you have done, rather it is something you are. Albert, you must know that some people resent you because of your background."

Albert thought he was not hearing right. "My background? What has that got to do with my ability as a physicist? Besides, I gave up my German citizenship when I was only fifteen. And soon now I will be a Swiss citizen."

"That may help, but it was not your nationality I meant. Forgive me, but your religion is against you."

"My religion? But I—I have no religion. I believe only in a God who watches over all the universe, not one who cares what happens to a particular individual."

"Believe me, Einstein, I am sorry. But consider my position. You are Jewish. You are not even a Swiss citizen yet. How can I pass over a Swiss boy to appoint you?"

Einstein was shaken after the interview. It was the first time that anti-Semitism had actually touched him. He had been vaguely aware that such a thing existed in Germany. But to think that it also existed in more enlightened Switzerland was upsetting.

Mileva also was having trouble locating a position. She was not a Swiss citizen, either. And she was a Greek Catholic, although she did not take her religion too seriously. Worst of all, she was a woman. Almost no one in 1900 could take a woman physicist seriously.

Meantime Albert began making the rounds of the secondary schools. Surely here someone would be happy to employ a teacher with a certificate from the famous Polytechnic School at Zurich. But again he met evasiveness and could find nothing.

Then one day a technical vocational school in Winterthur notified him that they had a temporary position open for a teacher. At last he had a job. True, this was not the job he had always thought he would have, but it was something to do at least. And it paid. Now he could afford to start eating well again. He enjoyed teaching the boys, and they responded well to his firm discipline and his interest in seeing that they learned.

After the school term was over, Einstein answered a newspaper ad for a tutor. A teacher who ran a boarding school in the lovely resort town of Schaffhausen needed a tutor for two boys. Einstein was delighted to get the job and frequently hiked out to the waterfall on the Rhine with his two young pupils. On the way he would discuss physics and mathematics, using examples the boys could understand. His pupils learned easily and quickly. Perhaps, Albert thought, all they had needed was someone who was interested in them. If that were so, why didn't he tutor them in all their subjects? Einstein proposed this to the teacher who ran the school.

"Then you do not think, Herr Einstein, that these boys would do as well with someone else."

"They haven't, Herr Director, but I feel sure I could make them learn other subjects also."

"Enough, Einstein. I thought your certificate from the Polytechnic School meant you would teach as I wished. Since you question the methods of the other teachers—since you question my methods—you must leave."

Albert went back to Zurich, somewhat shaken by this abrupt dismissal. His certificate in mathematics and physics seemed to be leading him nowhere. In addition, necessary cramming for the final examinations had soured him on scientific work for this past year. During this year he had to worry about earning enough to keep eating, something that he had never had to worry about as a student. But at least his Swiss citizenship papers had come through. Now he would surely be able to get a job in a secondary school. But Einstein soon discovered that being a "paper Swiss" was not much better than not being Swiss at all.

The one hopeful event that dark year was that he began to work on scientific problems again. His first paper, "Deductions from Capillarity Phenomena," was accepted by the German magazine *Annalen der Physik*. No matter that he had not been able to get a job in physics—he was a physicist. He had had an article accepted in the leading technical magazine of the day! He was not to feel this glow of creativity again until his first son was born. His important papers still lay in the future, but the acceptance of this first paper made Albert Einstein feel that he *had* been right about his talents. He would now go on and consider the fundamental principles underlying all of physics. By the time he had been out of school five years, he had published ten papers—among them the first paper on the photoelectric equation and the first paper on special relativity.

At this time, the Swiss Federal Office of Patents in Bern was looking for someone who could read over the patent applications, analyze them, and write a clear explanation of the principles behind them. Director Haller of the patent office was having difficulty finding the right man. He was discussing this with his friend Herr Grossmann one evening when Grossmann's son Marcel came in. Marcel listened carefully.

"Herr Director," he said respectfully. "I know someone I think could do this for you. He holds a certificate from the Swiss Federal Polytechnic School and has already published his first paper. I went to school with him, and even then he could always help the rest of us out with clear explanations."

"I would like to meet this young man. Would he come to Bern to see me?"

"I am sure he would, Herr Director. I will let him know right away." And Marcel rushed off to Zurich.

Albert was astonished. "What could I do for the patent office? Marcel, you sometimes allow your enthusiasm to run away with you!"

"Albert, he is looking for someone to write explanations of inventions. You could certainly do this! It isn't physics, I know, but perhaps it might lead to a job in physics. And it pays enough—3000 francs he said—so you will be able to eat regularly."

Albert's eyes twinkled. "As I am fond of eating regularly, I see I will have to talk to this man. Up to now no one has seemed worried about my eating or not."

Albert returned to Bern with Marcel and went to see Director Haller. Haller asked a great many questions about Albert's scientific and philosophical interests.

"This certificate of yours from the Polytechnic School. I didn't ask young Grossmann, but I presume it is in electrical engineering?"

"No, Herr Haller, in the teaching of mathematics and physics."

Herr Haller raised his eyebrows. "Teaching, eh? Then how do you know that you can analyze patent applications and write the proper explanations?"

"I do not *know* I can do this, but it seems to me I could. I would certainly try hard."

Herr Haller laughed. "Well, I need someone who both tries hard and understands what he is doing. And your first paper seems to show that you know what you are doing." He noted Einstein's start of surprise. "After young Grossmann spoke about you, I looked it up. I am willing to take a chance on you if you are willing to take a chance on us."

"When would you like me to start?" Einstein asked quickly.

"The first of the month will be time enough. You will be able to get settled here before you start."

Shortly after Albert started work in the patent office, he moved from a single room to an apartment. Mileva, still with some misgiving, had agreed to marry him. "I am still not sure I am doing the right thing," she told Albert frankly. "We are so different, you and I. Our families, our personalities, our religion. It is just physics that we share. And now you will do your work, and I will be just a wife."

"Not just a wife—my wife, Mileva," Albert reminded her gently. "As for the religion—you know this means nothing to me. I am sure we will be happy. Perhaps you will be able to use part of your time to work on a problem."

"No!" Mileva shook her head. "I told you we were different, Albert. I cannot work that way. For me, it is either completely one thing or completely the other. I will be your wife, but I will have to give up the physics."

"Perhaps you will feel differently about your work later on," soothed Albert.

Mileva threw herself into her career as Albert's wife with as much energy as she had previously attacked physics. She scrubbed their small apartment until it shone.

"Albert," she scolded crossly. "Your books are always out of the bookshelves. And look at your violin music! How will you be able to find what you want when your friends come to play chamber music with you?"

"Leave it, leave it, Mileva. You make too much of it. See, I find the Mozart quintet quickly, like this." His eyes twinkled as he demonstrated. "And our friends come to see us and to make music—not to look at our apartment."

But Mileva was as stubborn as he was. "But *I* look at our apartment and I do not like to always have things all over. I do not ever finish before I must start again."

Most of the time the newly married couple got along well, however, and settled down in their new home. Musician friends came to play music and discuss music. Physicists came to discuss the latest happenings in science. For this was a time of many new discoveries in science. Albert was happy, for his job demanded little time and he could devote himself to his real work. He was fascinated by molecular theory and its relation to thermodynamics and soon followed up his original

40

paper on thermodynamics, published in 1902, with others. He published "Theory of the Foundations of Thermodynamics" in 1903, the year he was married. This was followed in 1904 by "General Molecular Theory of Heat." Both papers were published in *Annalen der Physik*.

Mileva now had an additional outlet for all her energy. Hans Albert Einstein was born in 1904 and she lavished much time and affection on the baby's care. Albert was proud of his small son and was happy to watch the baby when Mileva went out marketing. Unfortunately, he sometimes forgot that he was babysitting, and Mileva would return to find him deep in a calculation, not even aware that the baby was screaming. Other times, however, he would play his violin to the child, sometimes lullabies and sometimes one of the sparkling Mozart tunes that he himself so loved.

But for Albert, work soon became the most important thing. He was in a fever of discovery. He submitted his inaugural-dissertation to the University of Zurich in 1905 and followed this within the year with the initial work on the photoelectric equation and the initial paper on special relativity—three papers which were due to shake the world of physics: 1. "Concerning an Heuristic View of the Production and Alteration of Light"; 2. "The Motion of Suspended Particles in Static Fluids Conforming to the Molecular Theory of Heat"; and 3. "Electrodynamics of Moving Bodies" (the initial paper on special relativity).

My major question was: What general conclusions can be drawn from the radiation-formula concerning the structure of radiation and even more generally concerning the electromagnetic foundation of physics?

Albert Einstein, "Autobiographical Notes"

# What Is Light?

If you were to ask a child in kindergarten "what is light?" he would probably answer: "Everyone knows what light is." He might even tell you that light is what we see by, and that we get it by turning on an electric light. A child who had been out camping might volunteer that you could get light from a fire. But the kindergarten child would not be able to describe for you the nature of light. Six or eight years later, the same question might be answered: "Light is an electromagnetic wave. Something like a radio wave, I think." After learning some general science the child has learned enough to give you an answer that is true—at least part of the time.

Physics, up to the time of Albert Einstein, was able to give an answer that was true—part of the time. We shall see how physicists had decided what light was before the time of Albert Einstein, and also how the work he did changed their ways of thinking about it. For all physicists were aware that the most important problems in physics between 1800 and 1920 were: What is radiant energy? What is light? What is electricity?

In 1666, Sir Isaac Newton was attempting to improve lenses used in optical telescopes. He found that when he let sunlight pass through a prism, he observed "very vivid and intense colors" on the wall of the room. He concluded that ordinary "white light is a combination of many different colors of light. Today, we call the band of colors he found a *spectrum*. (We have also found that the type of colors in the spectrum depends on the material emitting—giving off—the light and the temperature at which it is emitted.) In a paper that he sent to the Royal Society in England in 1675, Newton suggested that perhaps light was made of many, many very small and very rapidly moving "corpuscles" (small bodies) that are given off by all objects that shine. This theory of light became known as the *corpuscular theory*. Many scientists in the seventeenth and eighteenth centuries supported it, if only because the great Sir Isaac Newton had proposed it. But during the nineteenth century, scientists found that this theory did not explain all the facts that were being discovered.

In 1801 Thomas Young showed that a beam of light is refracted (bent) as it goes from one medium, such as air, into another, such as water. He pointed out that this could not be explained by the corpuscular theory of light. However if light were actually a *wave* of some sort, this action would be easily explained. Young performed a series of experiments that seemed to prove that light really was a wave. Other scientists became interested in the problem of the nature of light. Experimental evidence for the wave theory began to accumulate. Foucault in 1850 showed that light travels more slowly in water than in air, exactly what would be expected if the wave theory was true. If the corpuscular theory had been true, light should have traveled more slowly in air!

In 1862 the great English physicist James Clerk Maxwell derived his famous electromagnetic equations. He found that the velocity of electromagnetic waves agreed closely with the already measured velocity of light. This suggested to him that light itself was a special type of electromagnetic wave. In 1887 Heinrich Hertz performed a set of experiments which showed without question that light was an electromagnetic wave. The world of physics heaved a sigh of relief. Physicists no longer had to worry over the nature of light. They could finally go on to other more important matters.

However, while doing these experiments Hertz had accidentally discovered a fact that eventually would lead to a new and completely different theory about light. He discovered that a spark traveling through air between two terminals traveled more quickly if light were shining on the terminals than when the terminals were in the dark. Other physicists began to study this strange action. It soon became clear that negative electricity was being transferred from one terminal to the other, from the negative terminal to the positive one. Experiments proved that the electricity was carried by negatively electrified particles. But what could these particles consist of?

At first it was proposed that these particles were actually molecules of the gas surrounding the terminals. Later workers suggested that molecules of the terminal metal might actually have "boiled off" into the area and be carrying the charge. These theories proved wrong, but they led directly to the discovery of the electron by J. J. Thomson in 1897. (An electron is the natural, negative unit of charge.) Lenard was able to show in 1900 that electrons move from one terminal to another when light falls on the terminals, thus causing the photoelectric current that Hertz had discovered thirteen years before. He also showed that the *energy* of the photoelectric current depended on the material and not on the light intensity.

Meanwhile, other physicists investigated other aspects of the electromagnetic theory of light. In 1880, L. Lorenz had suggested that any material that could bend light rays might do this because the material contained small charged particles. He stated that these particles might vibrate back and forth around a fixed position. Physicists describe this fixed position as the equilibrium position. Lorenz showed that if each particle vibrated at a different frequency (the number of times that a complete vibration takes place each second), the material would act as a prism and disperse (spread) light.

Planck, the German physicist, was studying the emission of heat from a perfect emitter. A perfect emitter of radiation is one that absorbs all the radiation (heat, light, radio waves, etc.) falling on it and then re-emits all the radiation. Such a perfect emitter is called a *blackbody*. Planck knew that the radiation emitted from the surface of an object depends only on the temperature of the emitter. It does not depend on the material forming the emitter. The wave length of the radiation emitted is the same for all materials at the same temperature.

In interpreting these facts, Planck could not make them fit

into the framework of classical mechanics. He therefore proposed a radical new theory. He proposed that the vibrating particles suggested by Lorenz actually caused both the absorption and emission of radiation. These particles had a set of discrete energy levels at which they could oscillate. Furthermore, he stated that when radiation is absorbed (or emitted) these particles jump from one energy level to another. The energy gained (or lost) through such a transition is gained or lost as a quantum of energy. This quantum (amount) is equal to $fh$, with $f$ the frequency and $h$ a necessary constant. The constant $h$ is now known as Planck's constant and appears in many physical formulas.

Planck's idea was a new and startling one. He had proposed a bold departure from classical physics. Many, many physicists held that his quantum theory had to be wrong—it was too different. Yet men of genius—Einstein, and later Summerfeld and Schrödinger—seized this idea and laid the foundation for statistical quantum mechanics on it. This was a radical change from Newtonian mechanics. Einstein says of the implication of Planck's work: "All of this was quite clear to me shortly after the appearance of Planck's fundamental work; so that, without having a substitute for classical mechanics, I could nevertheless see to what kind of consequences this law of temperature-radiation leads for the photoelectric effect and for other related phenomena of the transformation of radiation energy, as well as for the specific heat of (especially) solid bodies."

Einstein picked up this work of Planck and used it to explain the photoelectric effect. He agreed with the assumption that when light is traveling between objects, the light behaves as though it were the electromagnetic wave proposed by previous investigators. This had been confirmed by much of the work in optics up to this time. But, he reasoned, when light *interacts* with matter, it no longer behaves like a wave. When light is either absorbed or emitted by a material, the light is made up of tiny particles (quanta). These quanta correspond to the corpuscles of earlier theory. Each quantum has an energy equal to $hf$, where $h$ is Planck's constant and $f$ is the frequency of the light *wave.*

When light is absorbed by a material, Einstein assumed, the energy of one quantum is absorbed by one atom of the material. This additional energy from the light quantum allows an electron to escape from the material. It is the escape of many of these electrons when light is absorbed by the material that causes the photoelectric current. Einstein was thus able to explain why the *amount* of photoelectric current varied with the *intensity* of the absorbed light. In addition, Einstein showed why the kinetic energy (energy of a moving body) of the escaping electrons depended *only* on the material and *not* on the intensity of the light.

Einstein assumed that the whole quantum of energy ($h\,f$) was absorbed by the atom, but that a certain part of this energy was used by the electron in escaping from the material. Accordingly, he wrote:

$$E = hf - w$$

48

This equation is Einstein's photoelectric equation. He received the Nobel prize for developing it. The equation states that the energy of an electron escaping from a material (which can also be written as half the mass of the electron times the square of the velocity [$v$] at which the electron is moving) is equal to the energy carried by one quantum ($hf$) minus the energy lost ($w$) in escaping from the material. This lost energy is the work function of the material and actually can be written $hf_0$ where $h$ is Planck's constant and $f_0$ is the frequency of light below which an electron cannot escape. This frequency differs with each material. A more usual statement of this equation is:

$$\tfrac{1}{2}mv^2 = hf - w$$

As you remember, Lenard had demonstrated that the energy of the electrons depended only on the nature of the material emitting these photoelectrons. After Einstein set down his photoelectric equation it was simple to see why. The work an electron had to do to escape from the material determined how much energy it would have when it escaped. Below a certain frequency, the work function of the material was higher than the energy absorbed and the electron could not escape.

Einstein's genius lay in taking Planck's theory of the quantum of energy and applying it to light. Einstein was a theoretical physicist and did not do any of the experimental work that proved that his photoelectric equation was correct, and that it held for X-rays as well as for visible and ultraviolet light. However, Einstein with *this one equation* solved the problem of what light really was—a problem that physicists had been trying to solve for three centuries. It is hard to emphasize enough the importance of this equation to modern physics. At one and the same time, it showed that light really had a dual nature and it laid the foundations for statistical quantum theory. Einstein has often been called the father of atomic energy by people who are thinking of his relativity theories. It would be far closer to the truth to consider him the father of atomic energy because of this equation. The Nobel prize committee realized the true significance of this work, and they awarded Einstein the Nobel prize in 1921 for his work on photoelectricity!

In considering his work, remember that up to this time physicists felt that light was an electromagnetic wave. There were certain experimental facts which could not be explained on the wave basis—but there were even more that could not be explained if light was thought of as being composed of particles. Einstein proposed that light had a dual nature. He stated that it travels as a wave travels and therefore can have all the characteristics of a wave and satisfy all the experimental evidence that had been found. But when light interacts with matter, the light is composed of particles and must be considered this way. Today we call the particle of light a *photon* to distinguish it from the quantum of energy it carries. We also know that all radiant energy, radio waves as well as light, behave in this manner.

As mentioned, this work laid the foundation for statistical quantum theory. Many physicists worked on developing quantum mechanics. Among the most famous are Schrödinger, Heisenberg, Dirac, and Born. Interestingly enough, Einstein never accepted statistical quantum theory as the final word. In his "Autobiographical Notes," he wrote:

"It is my opinion that the contemporary quantum theory by means of certain definitely laid down basic concepts, which on the whole have been taken over from classical mechanics, constitutes an optimum formulation of the connections. I believe, however, that this theory offers no useful point of departure for future development. This is the point at which my expectation departs most widely from that of contemporary physicists."

It was Einstein's dissatisfaction with statistical quantum mechanics that eventually led him to work on gravitation.

The agreement of these considerations with experience together with Planck's determination of the true molecular size from the law of radiation (for high temperatures) convinced the skeptics, who were quite numerous at that time (Otswald, Mach) of the reality of atoms.

Albert Einstein, "Autobiographical Notes"

# Molecular Theory

Einstein's paper on light interactions broke away from classical mechanics. His papers on Brownian motion, however, were based on classical mechanics. Einstein had posed himself the question: How can I determine theoretically that atoms of a definite, finite size really exist?

Einstein was not familiar with the work on statistical mechanics that Gibbs had published in 1901, and in 1902 independently worked out both statistical mechanics and a molecular-kinetic theory of heat. Einstein then set to work to prove that this molecular-kinetic theory of heat was correct and that molecules did exist. Indeed, the dissertation for which the University of Zurich granted him the Doctor of Philosophy degree in 1905 dealt with a method for determining molecular dimensions.

Einstein went on with this work and in 1905 published a paper on "The Motion of Suspended Particles in Static Fluids According to the Molecular Theory of Heat." He wrote this paper to demonstrate "that, according to the molecular-kinetic theory of heat, bodies of microscopically visible size suspended in a liquid will perform movements of such magnitude that they can be easily observable in a microscope, on account of the molecular motion of heat." In this paper he added also that these movements were perhaps identical with the motion known as Brownian motion.

Robert Brown, an English botanist, had observed in 1827 that very small particles suspended in a liquid are continuously in a state of motion. Einstein pointed out that the kinetic theory of heat predicts these continuous motions since the theory assumes that the molecules of the liquid are perpetually in motion—motion ceasing only at absolute zero, —273° Centigrade. The molecules of the liquid move in a random way and would have to hit the very small particles suspended in the liquid, thus making them move continuously.

In this first paper, Einstein showed how the effects of this molecular motion could be seen. He also pointed out the statistical nature of the motion; that is, that the theory could predict that the motion had to exist but could not predict what would happen to a particular molecule at a particular time. He worked out a relation between the Brownian motion of a particle and the number of molecules in a gram molecular weight of a fluid. The number of molecules in a gram molecular weight of a fluid is known as Avogardro's number; chemists had been using this number successfully for years. Einstein's relation was used by Perrin in determining Avogardro's number, and the results agreed with the determination obtained by more conventional ways.

Einstein wrote a second paper on Brownian motion in 1906.

By this time experimentalists were observing Brownian motion and were certain that it was caused by the motion of the molecules, as Einstein had predicted. Einstein worked out certain additional details in other papers, but he had done the trail-blazing work in the 1905 papers. Other men could work out the fine points of the theory. He had pointed out a new road, now let physicists travel it as they would. He himself had become interested in other and more startling concepts.

Physicists did travel this road; and as they traveled, they became convinced of the reality of atoms and molecules, paving the way for much we now know and have—from atomic energy to dacron and nylon. Einstein's contribution to quantum theory has already been mentioned. His mathematical development of Brownian motion convinced other physicists that probability plays a great part in the operation of the natural laws. This also led to the viewpoint of quantum mechanics, a viewpoint Einstein never shared. He always felt that physicists used probability only to cover their ignorance of how to handle numerous particles at one time.

From the very beginning it appeared to me intuitively clear that, judged from the standpoint of such an observer, everything would have to happen according to the same laws as for an observer who, relative to the earth, was at rest.

Albert Einstein, "Autobiographical Notes"

# *Special Relativity*

Even at sixteen Einstein had puzzled over the speed of light and the speed of material objects. The time he might have devoted to studying for his entrance examinations at Zurich he spent in considering the following problem: Suppose I could travel as fast as light. If I set out after a light beam, then the light should look like an electromagnetic field at rest. But he knew that such a thing was not physically possible. To solve this problem, Einstein felt, one *had* to assume that the same physical laws would hold for an observer in motion as held for an observer at rest. This was essentially what he was to hold later on, but he then had the mathematical tools to examine his assumption.

From the time Newton had written his work on mechanics, people "knew" that the length of a measuring device, such as a yardstick, was constant. They also "knew" that it was possible to state whether two events occurred simultaneously by observing the time at which the events occurred. For example, suppose a person is watching a jet travel through the air. At a certain point in the sky, the jet enters a patch of clouds. The person on the ground notes the time his watch shows. The jet pilot notes the time *his* watch shows. Assume that the watches are identical and that they were synchronized before the jet took off. What time does each watch indicate? You might guess that the watches would indicate the same time. However, Einstein's Special Theory of Relativity indicated that *relative to the watch on the ground* the moving watch in the jet must run more slowly.

Actually, however, the difference between two such watches would be too small to detect just by looking at the watches. Einstein, however, pointed out that atoms are natural clocks, since each atom vibrates at a definite rate common to all atoms of that material. If a set of such atoms then were made to move with a speed approaching the speed of light, it should be possible to see whether the natural frequency of the atoms were slowed down slightly. A physicist with the Bell Telephone Laboratories, H. Ives, carried out such an experiment in 1936. He confirmed the results that Einstein had predicted. Relative to a clock at rest, an identical moving clock runs more slowly!

Einstein went on to point out that even the human heart could be considered a clock, since it beats steadily. The heartbeat is often referred to as a clock. When the clock moves along with the person, it moves more slowly, relative to the same clock at rest, and the heartbeat apparently slows down. However, when the beat of the heart is measured by a clock moving *with* the person the beat is the same as when the person is at rest. All the body processes of an astronaut when he is in orbit for example, go on more slowly, relative to an observer on the ground. So an astronaut "ages" less in flight

But remember that this is aging less relative *only* to observers on the ground! Relative to any clock, including his heart, that the astronaut carries he ages at the same rate he did before.

Einstein was also able to show that a moving yardstick changes its length relative to the same yardstick at rest. He proposed therefore that all statements of time and distance carry the specification *relative to the particular frame of reference* used to make the measurement. It was his insistence that these measurements were relative that lead to his theory being called the Special Theory of Relativity.

By 1900, physicists had become fairly well convinced that the electromagnetic theories of Maxwell and Hertz were correct. Certainly they had predicted many effects which afterward had been observed. Ever since the days of Newton, scientists had talked about the ether. This was imagined to be an invisible, perfectly elastic medium which was supposed to fill all space. Light waves were thought to travel in the ether; for experience, as well as "common sense," told the scientists that waves—such as water waves and sound waves—had to travel in a medium. Light traveled in the ether. Light waves traveling in the ether, then, had to move with a definite velocity *relative* to the ether. Also, their velocity relative to material bodies in the ether changed. This reasoning was based on the statements Newton had made in his original work on mechanics. Newton's basic premises had been that absolute motion is the moving of a body from one absolute place to another, and that time flowed uniformly on and was the same no matter where it was measured.

Once the electromagnetic wave theory of light had been accepted, however, difficulties arose with this simple viewpoint. If the velocity of light waves in the ether relative to moving bodies had to change, then the apparent focal length of a telescope should change as the earth's orbital motion changed (as the earth moved through the ether). But this change had never been observed. This discrepancy led Fresnel to propose that perhaps a moving transparent body, such as a telescope lens, might in some fashion drag the light waves with it.

Fresnel's proposal seemed to solve the problem for a time. But every time a new theory is proposed, experimental physicists try to prove it. Michelson invented the interferometer so that he would have a sensitive enough instrument to measure any effect such as Fresnel had suggested. In 1887, Michelson and Morley performed their famous experiment, measuring the velocity of light along two paths, one in the direction of rotation of the earth and the other in the direction opposite this rotation. They could find no difference in velocity of light along the two paths! They repeated the experiment at different times of the day and at different times of the year. If there had been any motion of the earth through the ether, these velocities should have been different. The conclusion was inescapable; there was no motion of the earth relative to the ether.

There matters stood in 1905. A number of reasons had been advanced to explain why the motion would not have been observable, but upon examination none of these reasons fitted all the known facts. The explanation that was felt to be closest to the truth was the one given by the Dutch physicist, Lorentz. He stated that, in some undetermined manner, the earth's motion through the ether made the material of the interferometer shorten in the direction parallel to the earth's motion. This would cancel the effect of the earth's motion, and no effect would be observed. Lorentz tried to find a good theoretical reason why this had to occur, but he was never very successful. Still, he had offered a reasonable explanation and most scientists accepted it. To have done otherwise would have meant re-examining the basic principles of Newtonian relativity—something that occurred to no one. No one except Albert Einstein.

Einstein went back to the mechanics of Newton. He then proposed, in his most famous paper of 1905, that the entire concept of motion through the ether was meaningless. He stated that only motion of a body relative to another material body has any physical meaning. Hence the term relativity. He called this first paper "The Electrodynamics of Moving Bodies."

Newton's first law of motion, often called the law of inertia, states that bodies at rest will remain at rest unless disturbed by a force, and bodies in motion will remain in uniform motion unless acted on by a force. Einstein decided that this law of Newton's was the key to the problem. In this paper he based his arguments on two assumptions:

1. The velocity of light is constant and independent of the motion of its source.

2. The laws governing all physical events (both macroscopic and microscopic) are the same when observed by either of two observers in two different inertial systems. These laws can be stated relative to either of the systems but *never* involve motion of an ether, only motion of material bodies.

The constancy of the velocity of light had now been established by many astronomical observations. Newtonian mechanics, however, had predicted that if light came to us from an astronomical object moving toward us, the light should move with greater speed than if the object were moving away from us. For many years, it was not possible to measure the velocity of light accurately enough to prove, or disprove, this prediction. Once the measurements became possible, astronomers measured the velocity of light coming from each of a pair of double stars. As these stars rotate about each other, one star comes nearer to the earth and the other star moves away from the earth. Great was the surprise and consternation when it was found that light from each of these stars was traveling at exactly the same speed! Additional observations on other pairs of double stars, and on bodies such as comets that first move toward the sun and then away, confirmed this. Light travels with a constant speed and is not affected by the velocity of the source!

Astronomers and physicists proposed that constancy was only apparent, but none of the reasons given were completely plausible. It was as though they were saying, "our observed results do not agree with our theory, therefore our observations are wrong for some unknown reason. When we understand what is wrong with the way we made these observations, theory and observations will agree."

This assumption is not quite as arbitrary and foolish as it sounds. Some effects in physics need very delicate instrumentation to detect. And if certain effects, such as the shortening of the measuring instrument proposed by Lorentz, were true, it might *never* be possible to design experiments that could confirm the theory.

It was part of the genius of Albert Einstein that he abandoned this approach. He assumed that light had to be constant in velocity, regardless of the motion of the source. He went on to examine his second assumption also. The mathematics that he used were complicated, and we shall not try to explain them.

Albert Einstein's work on photoelectricity convinced physicists that Planck's quanta had a certain physical reality, and laid the foundation for quantum mechanics. His work on thermodynamics and Brownian motion convinced physicists of the reality of molecules, atoms, and the molecular-kinetic theory of matter. Most physicists would be pleased to have written one such fundamental paper in a lifetime. Two such papers, separated even by twenty or thirty years, would have proved the man a scientific genius indeed. But Albert Einstein wrote these two papers within a single year—and then he had gone on to relativity!

That the special theory of relativity is only the first step of a necessary development became completely clear to me only in my efforts to represent gravitation in the framework of this theory.

Albert Einstein, "Autobiographical Notes"

# The Young Professor—
# Zurich and Prague

Einstein published one more paper in 1905, called "Is the Inertia of a Body Dependent on its Energy Content?" This paper continued the ideas he had first expressed in his electrodynamics paper. Throughout the next few years the incredible outpouring of papers continued. Physicists began to come to Bern to meet this patent clerk who was doing such revolutionary work with such seeming ease. They began to urge that he be appointed to a professorship at the University of Zurich. Professor Kleiner himself, the most famous man in the physics department, came to Bern to see Einstein.

Mileva was overjoyed when she heard that he had come. She had always wanted to go back to Zurich; perhaps there would soon be a chance. She could hardly wait until Albert came back from the meeting.

"What did he say, Albert?"

"He said that everyone at the university was interested in my work and that he hoped that someday I could teach there."

Mileva was disappointed. "He came all the way from Zurich to say that? Albert, you are teasing me. What did he say— actually?"

Albert's eyes twinkled a bit. It was such fun teasing Mileva;

she always reacted so violently. Even if she became angry afterward he could rarely resist. "Actually, he advised me to become a *Privatdozent* here so that he could consider me if an opening came up."

(In the United States there is not an equivalent position. A *Privatdozent* taught at a university and held his lectures as often as he wished. He was not paid by the university and had only the very small fees that the students paid to attend the lectures. So a *Privatdozent* had to have some other way of supporting himself. Einstein, of course, was making an adequate salary at the patent office at this time.)

"You will, of course?" Mileva asked. She could see the streets of Zurich once again. She sometimes felt she had been happier there than she had been since, even with the baby.

"Perhaps," Albert replied. With that she had to be content.

Albert soon began to give the necessary lectures, although he never really enjoyed them. His idea of teaching was to go over a subject with one or two interested people, not to lecture before a group. He was still in the midst of his epoch-making discoveries and he often arrived at the lecture hall without knowing quite what he was going to lecture on. All too often his students were confused. Professor Kleiner came to hear him lecture and was somewhat disturbed by this.

"Dr. Einstein, it seems to me that you are not helping these students. This lecture was for professors, not for students."

Einstein shrugged. "Perhaps so. I had not thought about it."

"You should. If you continue to lecture on this basis I do not know that I can recommend you for a professorship."

Einstein laughed. "That's up to you. My more important work is my research. I can do this while I work at the patent office."

During these years Einstein was examining the various deductions derived from the Special Theory. In 1907 he wrote three papers on the Special Theory, using the term "relativity principle" for the first time in a title. The third paper is of particular interest to us today because in it he stated that the inertial (uniformly moving) mass of a physical body increases with an increase in kinetic energy. This led him directly to the equation $E = mc^2$, where $E$ is the total energy of a body, $m$ is the inertial mass of that body, and $c$ is the velocity of light.

This equation indicated that a very small mass, traveling at the velocity of light, could be transformed into a very large amount of energy. Astronomers were then able to account for the energy given off by the sun by showing that hydrogen atoms were transformed into helium atoms in the sun. Although a very small amount of solar mass is lost in this process, the sun radiates a very large amount of energy. Once atomic fission had been achieved, about thirty years after Einstein had published this paper, this equation also indicated that a terrifyingly destructive bomb was possible.

In 1909 the post of professor of theoretical physics became open at Zurich. Einstein had been recommended for the post and so had his old friend Friedrich Adler. The board of education of the canton of Zurich favored Adler because his father was a famous Social Democrat in Austria. When Adler heard that the board was considering appointing him rather than Einstein, he became incensed. He wrote a letter to the board stating that Einstein was much the better physicist, and that Adler felt the appointment should be divorced from the political scene. Adler convinced the board, and Einstein was offered the chair of physics at Zurich. The salary he was offered was no more than he had been getting at the patent office in Bern, but the position carried more prestige. Einstein accepted the appointment and the family made arrangements for the move to Zurich.

Mileva was overjoyed about the move back to Zurich. Here she had been happy. Here she would be happy again. She would have their second child in the city she liked best. And now Albert was a professor. Even though she had not been able to go on with her physics, even though the professors had ignored her talents, they could no longer ignore her as a person. For she was Frau Professor Einstein—the wife of Professor Einstein. Albert laughed at her delight in his new title.

Things were not easy for the young couple. They now had two children. Though Einstein had great respect from his colleagues, he and Mileva still had to manage on the same amount of money they had received in Bern. And Zurich was much more expensive than Bern.

Mileva had come from a section of Europe where poverty was common. She remembered all the tricks she had ever heard of and made filling cabbage soups and dark bread rather than the gugelhopf (coffee cake baked in a round mold resembling a Turk's turban) and spiced würst (sausage)

68

that Albert had loved from childhood. But it didn't help. Expenses mounted, but their income remained steady.

"Albert, I can't stand it any longer," Mileva complained one day. "I can now make one franc do the work of two— but to do the work of three or four, that is impossible."

Albert looked up from his desk, sighing. It was so hard to pull himself away from his work to notice these things. But as he looked at his wife, he realized that she had become much thinner and deep lines had appeared on her forehead. "Why she must have been giving me most of her own food," Albert thought suddenly. "And I never realized it before," he reproached himself. When he spoke, his voice was gentle.

"You like Zurich, Mileva. I am sorry that life is so hard for you just now, but perhaps next year there might be more money."

The following year, in the fall of 1910, Einstein was offered the chair of theoretical physics at the German University in Prague. This was a full professorship, and there would finally be adequate money if Einstein accepted it. But it would, of course, mean leaving Zurich. Once more Einstein talked it over with Mileva.

"I have been invited to become professor of theoretical physics at Prague, Mileva. A full professorship—with more money, also. We would be able to live comfortably again."

"In Prague? But Albert, to have to leave Zurich! We have been back barely a year."

"I know, Mileva. But Prague is, after all, in Austro-Hungary. Wouldn't you like to live in your homeland again?"

"No." Mileva's voice was bitter. "Austro-Hungary was never my homeland—not even when I lived there as a child. Now my home is here, in Zurich. I am a Swiss citizen. I would never willingly go back to the country that oppresses my people so!" In Mileva's statement, Albert could hear the echo of the age-old hatred of Slav for Magyar and German. Mileva's bitterness would make it harder for them if they went.

"I will have to state the church I belong to before they appoint me," Albert went on.

"You—belong to a church? You have often told me you believe all organized religion to be wrong."

"I do. I believe only in the sanctity of life. That is the Jewish belief—if a man leads a good life and is good to his fellow men, then he is holy. And that is what I believe. But if I must say I belong to a church, I will say I am Jewish. Can such a statement hurt me?"

So the Einsteins moved to the lovely old city of Prague. Mileva was still somewhat resentful of the fate that took her so far away from what she considered her "homeland," but Albert was looking forward to meeting his new colleagues. He had been told that a new professor always made calls on others of the faculty. He decided that this was a good way both to explore the city and to pay the formal visits expected of him. Although he picked the faculty members he called on in alphabetical order, he visited only those who lived in a section of Prague he was interested in seeing. And even then, he had made barely half the visits he might have when he became interested in some new work he was doing. He became convinced that these formal calls were a nuisance, regarding them as a complete waste of time. What had he to say to a professor of classical languages, for example—he who had hated Latin and Greek at the gymnasium? He decided abruptly to pay no more calls and was never aware that those faculty members on whom he did not call were insulted.

But if some of his colleagues were offended by his lack of formality and ceremony, his students were charmed by it. Unlike many of the other professors, Einstein always had time for special conferences in his office. "Never feel you interrupt me," he told some students who apologized for coming to see him. "I can always go back to my work after you leave. I want to hear what you think about your problems. Always feel free to come to see me."

The Germans in Prague at that time were about five per cent of the total population, but fully half of these Germans were Jews. Many of the German organizations, such as concerts, were strongly supported by the Jews. The Jews of Prague welcomed Einstein, and for the first time he became a member of a Jewish community that strongly identified itself with the fate of the Jews, rather than with that of other peoples. For age-old enmities still persisted in Prague and Jews remembered oppression even though their fellow Jews in Germany and Switzerland felt that persecution was a thing of the past. Many of the intellectuals among this Jewish group were Zionists. They felt that Jews as well as other peoples should have a homeland, and that their homeland should be the ancient Zion, then Palestine. Einstein was stimulated by their ideas, but did not become a Zionist until later.

Einstein had been trying to devise a theory of gravitation that would be simple, would take into account all the effects that had been observed, but that would still fit within the framework of the Special Theory of Relativity. But he had had no success. Finally he decided that the Special Theory was not applicable to gravity because of what he called "the principle of equivalence of gravitational forces and inertial forces."

Einstein pointed out that this new principle could be verified by astronomical observations. According to Newtonian mechanics, gravity would have no effect on a ray of light. According to Einstein, a light ray could be deflected (changed slightly in direction) by a gravitational field. The velocity of light is so great, however, that the effect of such a field would be very small—impossible to measure on the earth. But Einstein thought that the gravitational field of the sun might be strong enough so bending of light coming from stars could be seen. He calculated that the field of the sun would be strong enough to deflect the light ray toward the sun. Einstein himself suggested that it would be desirable for astronomers to check his calculations during a total solar eclipse. He had calculated that a ray of light coming from a star should be deflected from its path by 0.83 seconds of arc.

Astronomers were very much interested in Einstein's conclusions, but were not able to check them for a number of years. Total solar eclipses are rare and do not necessarily occur over observatories. The one German expedition that set

72

out to Russia to make observations were imprisoned there when World War I broke out.

It seemed to Einstein that someone always wanted him to do something. People didn't leave him alone so he could get on with his work. And now Mileva was talking of Zurich again. Perhaps he should not have told her that he had been offered the professorship in theoretical physics at their old school, the Swiss Federal Polytechnic School. But she asked for news every time he received a letter from Switzerland. And now he had to make up his mind about moving again.

"Have you decided yet, Albert?" Mileva asked him one evening after dinner.

"Not yet. It is lovely here in Prague. I can work here as well as anywhere, Mileva. And it is such a bother, all this moving around."

"But I don't work here as well as anywhere, Albert," she informed him. "Even if it is only housework these days, why must I do it in such a city? And you would not have to be bothered with moving. I will take care of everything."

Albert saw that she was determined. For him, it mattered little. He had made friends here; he had students and assistants. But Mileva became more and more unhappy. After all, what did it matter? As he had told her, he could work anywhere. They would go back.

True to her word, Mileva did all the work, consulting him only when she needed advice. She came to him one day with his uniform. Like others appointed to an Austro-Hungary government post, he had been obliged to buy a uniform to wear when he took his oath of allegiance to the emperor.

"Albert, what shall we do with this uniform? Perhaps Professor Frank would like to buy it from you when he comes. You have only worn it once. He would probably not object to buying it to wear once also."

Hans Albert was thrilled by the uniform. Why had no one told him of this before? He lifted the sword and pretended to swing it. "Papa, please. Before you sell the uniform, put it on and come for a walk with me. I want everyone to see how splendid you look."

Mileva started to scold the boy, but Albert intervened. "Let him alone. I can please my son that much. And perhaps," here his eyes twinkled, "perhaps they will think that I am an admiral in the Brazilian Navy."

Philipp Frank did want to buy the uniform and he, too, wore it only once. He tells the tale in his book about Einstein, adding that eventually he gave the coat to a Russian general who arrived in Prague as a refugee after the Russian Revolution. The Russian, however, was not impressed by the fact that it was Einstein's coat. He was interested only in the fact that it was a thick, warm coat.

So the Einsteins moved back to Zurich once more. Einstein was now a famous person and many people wanted to meet him and to invite him and Mileva to their homes. But Einstein felt more comfortable with people he had known before, such as Marcel Grossmann. These people he could talk to and they understood what he was trying to do.

"So I am convinced, Marcel," Albert stated one night, "that

74

one of the reasons I have not yet been able to deal satisfactorily with gravitational forces is that I do not have the proper mathematics yet. Pick thought—did you ever meet Pick, by the way? Well, no matter. Pick thought that I should look into the work that Ricci and Levi-Civita have done. But so far I have not had time to do so."

"I have done something with their ideas myself," Marcel mentioned diffidently. "If you would like to discuss them sometime, perhaps I might be of some help."

"Excellent, Marcel. Come, let us make a start now. Mileva, we are going to my study to work. We are not to be disturbed, but perhaps you could bring us some coffee later."

Einstein led the way out of the room, unaware of the resentful way Mileva was staring after him. It was always this way, she thought bitterly. Friends came, and they always ended up in the study. She might as well be a servant. All she was good for was to bring coffee in later, but not to disturb the great men at their work—no, never that.

That night was the first of many that Einstein spent with Marcel Grossmann, discussing the mathematics that might make his work easier. Finally he published a paper with Grossmann dealing with the relationship between a general relativity theory and a theory of gravitation. In the fall of 1913 he delivered a paper in Vienna, at the 85th Congress of German Scientists, in which he discussed many of his ideas on the problem. It was on this trip to Vienna that he met Ernst Mach, the philosopher-physicist whose ideas had greatly influenced the young Einstein.

The eminent heuristic significance of the general principles of
relativity lies in the fact that it leads us to the search for those
systems of equations which are *in their general covariant* formulation the *simplest ones possible;* among these we shall have to
look for the field equations of physical space. Fields which can be
transformed into each other by such transformations describe the
same real situation.

Albert Einstein, "Autobiographical Notes"

# The Berlin Years

The Einsteins were busy setting up housekeeping in Zurich again. Meanwhile, Max Planck and Walter Nernst, the leading German physicists of the time, were persuading the head of the Kaiser Wilhelm Institute in Berlin that Albert Einstein should be invited to Berlin. After Adolf Harnack understood the significance of Einstein's work, he was glad to issue the invitation. Planck and Nernst, both Nobel prize winners, personally went to Zurich to see Einstein.

"You know, Einstein, how important we in Berlin consider your work. Now, we would like to set up a research institute for physics at the Kaiser Wilhelm Institute and we would be happy if you would become the director," Nernst announced.

"But my dear Nernst, I am simply a theoretical physicist. I am not an administrator. You, yourself, are more suitable for such a position. You not only understand physics, you also understand people. I must admit that I am often astonished at what people will do when you ask them a simple question."

"You don't understand, I see. We have no money for building such an institute now, nor are we likely to have in the future. But we will organize it and you will be the director. If we have no institute, then the director will have to do something with his time. Perhaps work on the theory of gravitation that you talk about so often."

Einstein laughed. "Nernst, they always said you had a good business head. It is true, I did not understand. Nor do I understand one more thing. Just how will this non-existent institute be able to pay a director if there is no money?"

This time Planck answered. "We also have an invitation for you to join the Royal Prussian Academy of Science. The membership which we offer you carries with it a large salary. And you would be asked only to organize the research in physics, both at the Academy and at the Institute.

"We have not finished yet," Planck went on. "We at the University of Berlin would also like to have you as a colleague. So we are inviting you to become professor of theoretical physics there. You may lecture as often, or as little, as you wish. You may have as many, or as few, students as you wish. You will not have to do administrative work—not even in the giving of exams. We know that you dislike this sort of task. You will be free to do your own work. We ask only that you discuss the results with us, so that we can take it into account in our own work."

"Yes, you tempt me very much," Einstein remarked. "But you know I have only recently returned from Prague. Let me consider this a bit."

Attractive as the offer was, Einstein was not certain that he really wanted to return to Germany. He had fled from there as a youth, mainly repelled by the militaristic and regimented outlook. Did he want to go back now, at thirty-four, to Berlin?

78

For Berlin had always been the stronghold of the Prussian Junkers, the military class that represented everything Einstein hated. Yet it was undeniable that Berlin was also the scientific and mathematical center of Europe. It was a hard decision to make. Especially hard since he realized that Mileva would probably hate Germany. She was unhappy in Prague, he thought uneasily. What will she say when I mention Berlin to her? Yet he knew he would tell her of the offer that night.

"You are not considering taking this offer, Albert?" she asked.

"Yes, of course I am considering it. Not often does one get such a generous offer. Berlin is the scientific center of Europe. How can I turn such an offer down?"

"You drive me to this, Albert," her voice was so low he could barely hear her. "I tell you outright I refuse to raise my sons in Germany. If you go, you must go alone."

"I didn't realize that you felt so strongly about it, Mileva. Well, time enough to discuss it again when I decide."

In the end Einstein decided to make the move. Mileva kept to her resolve not to go to Germany. So at the end of 1913 Einstein left without Mileva or the boys.

Once in Berlin, Einstein settled down to work again. He lectured occasionally on his theories, mostly to scientists but occasionally to lay audiences. He took part in the weekly physics seminar at the University of Berlin. Here every week the leading physicists in Berlin—which at that time meant almost all the outstanding physicists in Europe—met and discussed progress in physics and mathematics.

Einstein was working on a number of projects: He was still working out the relation of gravitation to relativity; he and de Haas had developed experimental proof that Ampere's theory of molecular current was correct; he was interested in the relationship between theoretical and experimental physics and wrote a paper on this. Einstein now was happily anticipating a long, quiet life of working and writing.

But a young student in Sarejvo shot and killed Archduke Francis Ferdinand and two months later, in August 1914, World War I started. Now the quiet life that Einstein had looked forward to was doubly upset. All his life he had been a pacifist—a deep believer in peace. In addition, he had insisted on keeping his Swiss citizenship when he returned to Germany. So here he was, a pacifist in a country that eagerly was going to war—and a citizen of a neutral nation living in one of the warring nations. Even if he had felt that the German cause was just, he would have been unhappy. But he strongly believed that if the Germans had not tried to dominate central Europe the war could have been avoided.

The war, he knew, meant that he might not be able to see his family until it was over. Now, more than ever, Mileva would refuse to come to Germany with the boys, even if she could leave Switzerland. And if he left Berlin to go to Switzerland, he might not be allowed to come back into Germany. His pessimistic outlook proved correct. He finally received a letter from Mileva stating that as things stood, it would be better for them to end their marriage. Einstein grieved, for he missed his home, and particularly his sons. But his work had always been most important in his life. Now he devoted himself to it even more.

When German troops invaded neutral Belgium, a great many people all over the world were astonished. When reports of German "atrocities" in Belgium began, the people of Western Europe were shocked. Everyone knew the splendid music of Beethoven, the lovely verse of Schiller, the philosophy of Kant. Surely these "Boche" who ground little Belgium under their heels could not belong to the same nation! So the groundwork was laid for the story of the two Germanys: the Germany of Schiller and the Germany of Bismarck.

In Germany, however, the truth was that most of the intellectuals supported the war effort. At the urging of the government, ninety-three of the outstanding writers, philosophers, and scientists signed the famous "Manifesto to the Civilized World." This manifesto stated that there was only one Germany, a Germany that was not guilty of the atrocities charged. It ended by stating that German culture had inevitably led to German militarism to defend it.

But a very few who loved German culture could not stand by! The pacifist Georg Friedrich Nicolai immediately wrote an answer: "Manifesto to Europeans." Nicolai was a professor in physiology at the University of Berlin. He passed his manifesto around to his fellow professors, asking them to sign. But only three men of the entire staff were willing to sign it with him. Albert Einstein was one of the three. It was the first public political statement Einstein made.

As the war progressed, food and clothing became scarcer.

Einstein, who rarely thought about such things when he was working hard, became ill. He had formed the habit of going once or twice a week to his Uncle Rudolf's apartment. His cousin Elsa, now a widow with two young girls, kept house for her father. She fussed over her cousin "Albertle," trying to persuade him to eat more. When Elsa and her father realized that Albert was ill, they insisted that he give up his room and move in with them.

Elsa's two young daughters were delighted with their "new" cousin. Except when he was too tired or too ill, he loved to play with them. He frequently played his violin for them, thinking often of how his mother had played for him. Elsa looked at the family table with affection one night. "Having Albert here has made a great deal of difference," she told her father softly.

Albert himself acknowledged the difference that Elsa made in his life when he asked her to marry him soon after that. They were married in 1916. Now he had a family again! A family with two daughters instead of the two sons he seldom saw. His new wife was a gentle person who easily accommodated herself to her Albertle's ways. There was no doubt in his mind that Elsa would follow him anywhere, as indeed she had to some years later.

The most important event in the war years was the publication in 1916 of Einstein's "Foundations of General Relativity." In this paper, he generalized from the Special Theory and completely and logically managed to include gravitation in the theory of relativity. This paper represented a much more radical break with classical (Newtonian) physics than the Special Theory. It is the General Theory that one thinks of when the statement is made that Einstein overthrew Newton.

The mathematical basis for the General Theory of Relativity is quite complex. No attempt will be made to give the mathematics here. You need only remember that the Special Theory dealt with the case where two systems (references) were either at rest relative to each other or moving with a uniform speed in a straight line relative to each other. The General Theory explained what happens when two systems move in other than straight lines and at speeds that can vary relative to each other. Thus, the General Theory was particularly good at explaining the motion of planets, comets, or other bodies that rotate.

In the General Theory, Einstein showed that space had to be both curved and finite; that is, that it has definite volume. However, he also predicted that space has no actual boundaries. In essence, what he said was that light in space travels along a closed curve, returning to its origin if not intercepted. The field laws he deduced from this theory state in what way the masses (stars, planets, and so on) produce curvature in space. His laws of motion show how geodesic lines (shortest distance between two points on a curved surface) can be found for any space whose curvature is known.

Most important of all, Einstein pointed out that it was possible to check the General Theory of Relativity experimentally. Three different and independent experiments could be used. We have already mentioned the deflecting of light toward the sun. He also showed that the motion of the planets had to be altered very slightly from what Newtonian mechanics would give. His calculation explained an observed discrepancy in the orbit of Mercury of 43.5 seconds of arc per century. The third experimental result would be that the spectral lines from an element in space should be redder than those from the same element on the earth. (Spectral lines are the lines seen when light given off by vibrating atoms is passed through a prism or, more usually, a diffraction grating.)

Einstein continued to work during the war years, content to wait for the tests of his General Theory. In 1917 he published the first edition of his book *Relativity, the Special and General Theory*, but the first authorized English translation was not published until 1920.

Then, on November 11, 1918, the guns fell silent. The Great War, as many people called it, was finally over. Germany and her allies were defeated.

Peace brought with it the opportunity to test Einstein's General Theory. Two English expeditions set out to photograph the total eclipse of the sun that would take place on March 29, 1919. The great astronomer Sir Arthur Eddington was in charge of the expedition that went to the island of Príncipe in the Gulf of Guinea, West Africa. Public interest ran high when the expedition came back. The photographs taken were carefully measured. On November 6, 1919, at a combined meeting of the Royal Society and the Royal Astronomical Society, the results were announced. Rays of light passing the sun are deflected in the sun's gravitational field by 1.75 seconds of arc, the amount predicted by Einstein's Theory of General Relativity. (Note that this amount is different from the amount originally predicted by Einstein.)

This announcement excited the general public and gave rise to a great deal of rather inaccurate speculation in the newspapers. In Germany, everyone was pleased that "German" science had been proved right on so radical a new theory. It took some of the sting out of losing the war. In England, however, the newspapers were busy showing just how un-German this "German" scientist really was. Einstein was disturbed by this as he felt that what he did should be appreciated for itself, not because he was (or was not) a German. Science, he felt, was not a matter of nationality. What did it matter if he were a German or a Swiss—a Jew or a Gentile?

But few people inside or outside Germany were willing to accept his viewpoint. The English continued to feel that he was more Swiss than German. The Germans continued to feel that he was more Jewish than German. This was simply a forecast of life to come. In only twelve years he would be forced to leave Germany because he was a Jew and his theory would be ridiculed as "Jewish Science."

My political ideal is democracy. Let every man be respected as an individual and no man idolized. It is an irony of fate that I myself have been the recipient of excessive admiration and reverence from my fellow. beings through no fault, and no merit, of my own.

Albert Einstein, *Ideas and Opinions*,
translated by Sonja Bargmann

# The Clouds Gather

After this first proof of the General Theory of Relativity, Einstein became even more famous than he had been. Reporters sought to interview him on all the important topics of the day. Learned men in various fields came to consult with him. Einstein regarded all the fuss with detachment and wry amusement. He continued to work on the things he considered important and ignored other things.

Now that the war was over, Einstein could get to Switzerland more often to see his first family there. Unfortunately, postwar inflation in Germany made it difficult to support the boys and Mileva as well as he would have wished. He was always glad to get home to Elsa, though. He had gotten used to having her take care of him. Since it was important to her, he managed to look right on special occasions, although he never quite understood why it was important. "People come to hear me lecture, not to look at me," he would complain when she scolded him for not dressing properly.

Elsa managed the household skillfully. "I don't understand my husband's mathematics," she told reporters who interviewed them on their first trip to the United States in 1921. "But I can add up our household accounts." It was Elsa who

87

saw that the household had enough food and clothing during the bad war years. It was Elsa who knew how to get the delicacies that were scarce even after the war. It was Elsa who arranged dinner parties for friends. Many of these friends were musicians who could play the Beethoven and Mozart melodies that her Albert loved so much. Music was still a source of great joy to him. Whenever he was bothered by a problem, he turned to his violin. In working out the intricate phrasing of a piece, he found new ability to go on. And from 1920 on, the problems that bothered him were more and more often political problems.

Many scientists in Berlin criticized Elsa as an oblique way of criticizing Einstein. They complained that she kept scientists from him and arranged that he meet only artists and musicians. They complained that she was not Einstein's intellectual equal. She admitted that cheerfully enough, saying, "I do not pretend to understand my husband's theories. It is more important for me to understand what he prefers to eat." If Einstein was disturbed by these attacks on his wife, he did not show it. He had chosen her; he was happy with her. If the rest of the world didn't approve, he was sorry but not about to change the life that suited him.

Einstein now received many invitations to lecture at universities and science meetings all over the world. He also lectured before the public, explaining his theories as simply as he could. Newspaper reporters followed him around.

Although most people treated him with respect, bordering almost on awe, a small group of Germans hated Einstein. To these people, it seemed inconceivable that the German military establishment had actually lost the war. How could this have happened when the entire world had admitted the superiority of the German army and navy? Other countries had even organized their armies after the German pattern. These people felt that the German army had never really been beaten but rather had been betrayed by weakminded politicians. It was much easier to look for scapegoats than to accept the truth.

One of the scapegoats was Albert Einstein. Here was a man who had been born a German but had become a Swiss citizen. Moreover, he was a Jew, which meant to their inflamed minds that he was capable of anything. In addition, he had refused to support Germany's war efforts, stating frequently that he felt the war was unjust. He had joined the *Bund Neues Vaterland* (the New Fatherland Association) during the war. The Bund worked for a just peace among all nations. Many of its members were socialists, and the press soon began to call Einstein a socialist. The activities of the Bund made it unpopular during the war. Afterward, because members accepted the fact that Germany had been beaten and not betrayed, the Bund became even more unpopular than it had been.

A strange thing now happened. Many of the newspapers that had been jubilant when English scientists had been forced to admit that the General Theory of Relativity had been proved, now turned on Einstein. He became an easy target for malcontents of every stripe. The reactionary papers accused him of being a "Bolshevik." The Communist papers, both in Germany and in Russia, accused him of being a reactionary bourgeois. Anti-Semitic papers kept pointing out that he was a Jew. In a personal letter to Max Born, the physicist, Einstein complained: "The Yellow Press and other half-wits are at my heels to the point where I can scarcely draw breath, let alone do any decent work."

Einstein at this time went to the University of Leyden in Holland to lecture. He was almost mobbed by a crowd of 1400 students who came out to hear him talk and cheered him wildly. The university appointed Einstein a professor of physics, whose only duties would be to deliver lectures at his convenience. Einstein was delighted with this arrangement. He welcomed visits to Leyden, which was always peaceful and where he was never attacked as he was in Berlin. His physicist friend Paul Ehrenfest, and Paul's wife, also a physicist, were in Leyden. They formed the nucleus of a group always willing to listen to Einstein and to discuss his ideas. Einstein always needed such a group of listeners. His students often learned more in conversation with Einstein than they did in his more conventional lectures. German papers began to question openly whether Einstein meant to leave Berlin and go to Leyden permanently.

To most German scientists, the thought that Einstein might leave Berlin was disturbing. They realized that he was the most eminent of that very eminent group. The government also realized that Einstein was valuable to Germany's reputation. The Minister of Education himself wrote to Einstein and begged him to ignore the unfair attacks on him and to remain in Germany. He reminded Einstein of the esteem in which he was held by the German Federal Republic.

Einstein was moved by this letter. Here was the government acknowledging him as a German scientist. He would certainly not desert Germany when he was needed to enhance German prestige throughout the world. He answered the letter immediately, stating that he was bound to Berlin by both human and emotional ties. He would certainly stay in Berlin if he were not driven out. Furthermore, Einstein stated, he would apply for German citizenship now that Germany was a republic.

In May of 1920 he received his first American honor. Columbia University awarded him its Barnard Medal for Meritorious Service to Science. Although he could not go to New York to accept in person, he sent a letter of acceptance.

In January of 1921, he went first to Prague, then on to Vienna. In Prague, he was met by his successor as physics professor, Philipp Frank. Frank worried over how he could ensure that Einstein would get the peace and quiet that he loved. Finally he had an idea. Frank himself had been married for only a few months. He and his wife had been living in Frank's office because they had not been able to find an apartment. If they moved to another room, Einstein could stay in his old office. Frank wondered if Einstein would have become too important to take this sort of accommodation. But when Einstein got off the train, clutching his violin case, Frank felt relieved. This was the same Einstein he had known—charming, humble, and witty. This Einstein was delighted to stay in the office.

The next night Einstein delivered a lecture to the Urania Association. As always when he lectured to the general public, he was simple, clear, and witty. Later that evening he was the guest of honor at the home of the chairman of the Urania Association. There he listened gravely to speeches lauding him and his principles. At last it was his turn to respond. He stood up and said quietly: "I think it will be more enjoyable and certainly more understandable if I play some Mozart for you, rather than making a speech." He played his violin quietly, communicating to those listening his joy in the crystal-clear tones.

Einstein went on to Vienna, where he stayed with Felix Ehrenhaft and his wife. Ehrenhaft was an outstanding experimental physicist at that time and his wife also was a physicist. Frau Ehrenhaft took over the care of Einstein's wardrobe while he stayed with them. Seeing that he had not brought bedroom slippers with him, she bought him a pair. But Einstein refused to wear them, preferring to go barefoot. He felt freer without slippers and would not be constrained by them. And when Frau Ehrenhaft got to Einstein's lecture she discovered that he was wearing his old baggy trousers, not the ones she had carefully sent out to be pressed. "A very great physicist and a very great man," she thought. "But what a trial he must be to his wife!"

While Einstein was in Vienna, he met Josef Breuer, the doctor who had co-authored with Sigmund Freud the first paper that laid the basis for modern psychoanalysis.

After Einstein returned to Berlin, he hoped that he could settle down to work again. And he did deliver a famous lecture on Geometry and Experience to the Prussian Academy shortly after returning. But Chaim Weizmann, the head of the General Zionist Movement, invited Einstein to go to the United States with him on a fund-raising trip.

Einstein had met Zionists in Prague but had never worked for the Zionist movement. Although he wished that he could foresee an end to nationalism, which he felt brought wars and suffering, he was realistic enough to know that this was not going to happen in his lifetime. Einstein himself had felt the sting of anti-Semitism, and he knew that Jews who had lesser talents had to battle great discrimination. Many Jewish students were turned away from colleges. Many Jewish college graduates were denied jobs because they were Jewish. These facts were known to Einstein. Now the Zionist movement was planning to found a university at which Jews, and others also, would always be welcome. Einstein had great hopes for the proposed Hebrew University in Jerusalem. Now Weizmann was inviting him to help raise money for it. How could he refuse?

Einstein and his wife sailed for New York and the American tour. They both loved sailing small craft, but this was the first transoceanic trip for either of them. When they landed in New York, they were beseiged by reporters and cameramen. Einstein tried to answer all the questions put to him. But when he was asked why he thought there was such excitement in New York over his coming, he laughed. "The ladies in New

York must have a new style every year—this year the fashion is relativity." Everywhere Einstein went people followed him, begging for autographs, trying to touch him, trying to talk to him. He never lost his sense of humor or sense of proportion.

Although the primary purpose of Einstein's visit was to help raise money for the Jewish National Fund and the Hebrew University, Einstein visited American universities. He met Michael Pupin, professor of physics at Columbia and discussed physics with him. He received an honorary degree from Princeton University and gave several lectures there on the theory of relativity. He visited the physics laboratory of Harvard University and discussed with the students, individually, the problems they were working on.

On the whole, Einstein was pleased with what he saw of the United States. Coming from a continent that had been torn by a great war, he was particularly impressed by the fact that people from many nations had settled in America and were living peacefully with each other. And he noticed that women in America played a much more important role in both public and private life than they did in Europe. But he was also impressed, unfavorably this time, by the willingness of most Americans to go along with the crowd. "In Europe," he remarked to Elsa, "we put a premium on the individual who dares to be different. Here he is pointed out and ridiculed."

Lord Haldane, an English statesman, persuaded Einstein to come to England on his way back to Berlin. Haldane was much interested in promoting better relations between England and Germany, and felt that Einstein could be of great help in achieving this end. Haldane himself introduced Einstein to the audience at King's College, who received him with much enthusiasm. Everyone seemed to want to meet Einstein. Even the Archbishop of Canterbury thought he had to talk with Einstein. The Archbishop, as the head of the Anglican Church, felt that it was his duty to understand the theory of relativity. Lord Haldane had told him that the theory had important meaning for contemporary theology. Nothing would do but his being invited by Lord Haldane to the dinner for Einstein. The Archbishop sat next to Einstein and carefully scrutinized this German Jew. Really, he did not look like anyone who could overturn religion. He looked more like some friendly musician, with his hair springing up from his head like that and his bow tie already slipping slightly. The Archbishop finally asked the question he had been pondering for weeks. "What effect does relativity have on religion?"

Einstein was somewhat startled. He had met all sorts of questions, some serious, some making fun of him. But he had never met one quite like that. But he could see from the Archbishop's troubled face that the question had been put seriously. "No effect at all," Einstein reassured the Archbishop. "Relativity is not concerned with religion. Religion does not need to be concerned with relativity." The Archbishop was relieved. He could now forget the books he had been studying and devote himself to his church administrative duties again.

The Einsteins got back to Berlin in June of 1921. They were both glad to be home, and the girls were delighted to see them. The household settled back into its daily routine. If everyone would leave him alone, Einstein thought, he might be able to get some work done again. He was trying to find some way of linking gravitational forces and electromagnetic forces. Einstein had always been certain that a very few fundamental ideas could be used to explain most of physics. Now he was attempting to find a way of fitting together forces that most other physicists thought distinct and different.

Summer was a time of special pleasure for Einstein, for then his sons came from Zurich to visit him. Hans Albert was interested in mathematics and wanted to become an engineer. Eduard, on the other hand, was the musician. He played the piano with considerable technical skill, particularly Bach and Mozart. But his musical insight was not as great as his father's and he frequently resented the suggestions that his father offered. "How strange," Einstein mused to himself as he listened to his son play. "He seems to enjoy playing, but it brings no calmness to him. He is much like Mileva, taking everything so seriously. Well, I do not know what I can do for him. He is taking it hard, this growing up. I can remember that it was hard sometimes to be young—but I at least knew what I wanted to do. The boy will just have to grow up, I suppose."

Dr. Bosch, head of I. G. Farben, the German chemical concern, felt that it was disgraceful that an important theory by a German citizen had had to be proved by an English expedition. He donated enough money to establish an institute to work with the Astrophysical Institute at Potsdam. This new institute built a tall tower, later called the Einstein Tower, from which to measure the color of the spectral lines from distant stars. In his General Theory Einstein had predicted that these lines would shift to the red end of the spectrum. Now astronomers set to work to measure this shift, and in 1924 they had completed observations that again substantiated Einstein's General Theory of Relativity.

Much as Einstein desired it, people would not leave him alone. He was soon invited to join the Committee on Intellectual Cooperation of the League of Nations. Marie Curie had also been invited to join, as had philosophers such as Henri Bergson. Elsa was much excited by this honor.

"Just think, Albert. You have been invited to be on this committee and Germany isn't even a member of the League. Perhaps this shows that the League will soon admit Germany."

"Perhaps." Einstein was inclined to be pessimistic. "Although it is an honor for me, personally, I am not sure that I should accept. What will the German papers think? They attack me and others now, because we are Jewish. And I don't know that I want to be thought of as a representative from Germany. Well, I must think about it."

But Einstein finally decided to accept. Perhaps, he thought, he could do something more to help the cause of peace to which he and Elsa were so devoted.

In France, meanwhile, Paul Langevin, the French physicist, persuaded the College of France to invite Einstein to Paris. Although this invitation was seconded by most people, there were some French scientists who could not think of Einstein primarily as a physicist. They thought of him primarily as a German. Ignoring Einstein's opposition to the war, they remembered only that Germany had invaded France. But in March, 1922, Langevin and former premier Paul Painleve were able to invite Einstein to Paris. They took unusual precautions to guard Einstein against hostile demonstrations. These included having Einstein leave his train station by a side exit to avoid a crowd of excited young people. Langevin safely got Einstein out of the station and to his hotel, avoiding the crowds—who turned out to be students waiting to welcome Einstein, with Langevin's son among the leaders! Einstein gave one public lecture on March 31, and a number of scientific lectures.

Einstein enjoyed his stay in Paris, and particularly enjoyed meeting Madame Curie and Henri Bergson.

By the time Einstein got back to Berlin, he was feeling more hopeful about the international scene. But in Berlin the domestic scene was worse than when he left. His friend Walter Rathenau had become foreign minister. The fact that Rathenau was Jewish inflamed the reactionaries, particularly those who had joined the new party called the National Socialist (Nazi) Party. Rathenau was frequently threatened, but he ignored the threats. On June 24, 1922, Rathenau was shot while riding in his car.

The Einsteins were shocked by the brutal assassination. Rathenau's only fault had been that he was Jewish. The papers openly speculated that Einstein might be the next to be shot, for he too was an internationally known Jew. The rumors frightened Elsa and she insisted that her husband work at home for a while. He gave in, but soon insisted on going back to his office. When a peace movement he had been active in organized a march for peace, Einstein disregarded all Elsa's pleas and joined the march. But the strain was beginning to tell on him, and he allowed himself to be persuaded to take a trip to the Orient beginning in the fall of 1922.

By the time Einstein arrived in Shanghai, he had received another honor. On November 10, 1922, he had been given the Nobel Prize in Physics "for the photoelectric law and his work in the field of theoretical physics." Although he was most famous for his relativity theories, relativity was not mentioned by name. Relativity was still an object of much derision for certain people, particularly those physicists who felt that all theories must be based on experimentation with material objects. The Swedish Academy felt its decision would be less controversial if the prize was awarded for a discovery from which mankind derived a great use. In setting up the prizes originally, Alfred Nobel had made "great use for mankind" the criterion. The Academy had to decide whether relativity was such a discovery or not. The members took the easier way out and awarded the prize for something more understandable and less controversial.

In justification, however, remember that Einstein's work in photoelectricity was of fundamental importance. From this work, Bohr went on to postulate a new theory of the atom. Prince Louis de Broglie, in his doctoral dissertation, introduced a viewpoint into mechanics that was analogous to the one Einstein had introduced into optics. Erwin Schrödinger developed from de Broglie's ideas a new "wave mechanics" that held within the atom. Little by little, what we now know as *atomic physics* developed from Einstein's photoelectric equation. Einstein himself was never happy over the viewpoints of the younger men. "I cannot believe that God shoots dice with the world," he would say when questioned about the new quantum mechanics. It is ironic that Einstein was awarded the Nobel prize for work that led to a new physics he never could agree with!

His trip through the Orient was a splendid triumph. Everywhere he went, crowds gathered to see him. The Einsteins were shocked, though, at the misery and poverty of the great mass of the people. They had thought that Europe had known suffering immediately after the war. In the Orient, the majority of the people could never hope for a life that was better than Europe's worst suffering. This made a great impression on the Einsteins, and they became even more interested in working for peace and the well-being of all mankind.

Japan, though, was charming. Einstein could not get enough of it. He was received by the Empress herself—a great favor to be shown a foreigner. He lectured to overflow crowds.

Leaving Japan, the Einsteins sailed back toward Europe. Einstein had worked and lectured for the Zionist cause. Now he had an opportunity to see Palestine himself. He was especially interested in seeing the site of the Hebrew University on Mount Scopus, with Jerusalem spread below. Einstein and his wife were much moved by this. Here would be a university that would be open to all, Jews and Gentiles alike. At long last, the "people of the Book," who so valued learning, would have an opportunity to absorb secular as well as religious teaching.

Tel Aviv was a new city being built on sand near the coast. Although much of the hasty building so far was of flimsy construction, the citizens had great hopes for the city. As Jerusalem was the spiritual center for Palestinean (and world) Jewry, Tel Aviv was destined to become the industrial center. Here, at last, the world would see a return for the Jews to the "normalcy" other peoples enjoyed. Due to the restrictions placed on Jews in Europe, they had been unable to own land or to pursue many of the jobs and professions open to others.

The Einsteins left Palestine in March of 1923, returning to Marseilles. But before they returned home, they went on to Spain. Here, too, Einstein was greeted with much enthusiasm. He had an audience with King Alfonso XIII and met many of the Spanish nobility. He toured the ancient universities. Einstein had a strong sense of history and remembered well that it was the universities of Spain, particularly under the Moors, that had saved the learning of Greece for the modern world.

While the Einsteins had been enjoying their six-month cruise, politics had gone on as usual in Europe. The League of Nations was proving unable to arbitrate quarrels between the great powers. The French government refused to submit the question of Germany's reparation payments to the World Court and instead sent troops into the Ruhr industrial area of Germany. Einstein was distressed by this move and after he returned from his trip resigned from the Committee on Intellectual Cooperation. In writing to the League, he stated: "I have become convinced that the League possesses neither the strength nor the sincere desire which it needs to accomplish its aims. As a convinced pacifist, I feel obliged to sever all relations with the League. I request that you strike my name from the roster of committee members."

In spite of his resignation, Einstein kept up an active correspondence with members of the pacifist movement in Europe. He felt strongly about all injustice. Before the war, he had attended all the scientific meetings organized by the Belgian industrialist, Ernest Solvay. Lorentz wrote to Einstein, asking if he wished an invitation to the new Solvay conference. Einstein felt strongly about the international aspects of science, and replied, ". . . . It would be wrong for me to take part in a meeting from which my German colleagues are excluded on principle. . . ." It was not until 1925, when German scientists were again invited to the Solvay conference, that Einstein attended.

In Munich in November, Adolf Hitler and his Nationalist Socialist Party friends attempted the unsuccessful Beer Hall Putsch. It was felt that Einstein's life once more was threatened. He left Berlin for Leyden, where he was always welcome, but returned before long. Meanwhile, he was having second thoughts about his resignation from the Committee on

Intellectual Cooperation. He finally indicated to the League that he would reconsider, and on June 21, 1924, the Secretary-General of the League issued a formal invitation to Einstein, which he accepted. He attended his first session on July 25, 1924.

In spite of all the political turmoil of those years, Einstein continued to work. Perhaps the most important paper he wrote at that time was the first paper on "A Unified Field Theory of Gravitation and Electricity." After doing further work, Einstein realized he had been on the wrong track in this paper and started looking for a new approach.

In the spring of 1925, he and his wife went to South America. Here he spoke to scientific meetings and met members of the Jewish communities. He discussed his Unified Field Theory with the scientists. To the Jewish meetings, he described Palestine as it had been when he saw it, and he again raised money for the Jewish National Fund. And everywhere he went the German communities welcomed him as a great German scientist. He knew that many of the members of these German communities were sympathetic to the Nazi cause, yet they welcomed him. He commented in his diary: "Strange people, these Germans. I am a foul-smelling flower to them, and yet they keep tucking me into their buttonholes."

He went back to Berlin, back to work, back to political turmoil, back to involvement in the cause for peace. About this time, Einstein became convinced that the only way of stopping war was for enough people to refuse to bear arms. He felt that if enough prominent people refused military service, others would follow, and peace would be secure. At the beginning, he felt, if two per cent refused to go into military service, world opinion would have to change. It was only much later, when he realized the character of the German Nazi and Italian Fascist parties, that he felt that certain wars could not be avoided.

In March, 1929, Einstein celebrated his fiftieth birthday. As the day drew near, letters, presents, and packages poured into his apartment. To avoid the newspapers, Einstein spent the day at the estate of a Berlin shoe-polish manufacturer. Elsa brought some of the packages he had received, and the Einsteins spent a quiet day. Elsa had prepared dinner at home and carried it along in picnic baskets. It was just the sort of quiet day Einstein liked best.

Among the gifts was a statement from the Zionist Organization in America informing Einstein that a plot of land in Palestine had been bought in his honor. Trees were being planted there, and the land would be known as the Einstein Forest.

Einstein loved sailing—it was the only sport in which he would take part. He had had a small boat, bought third- or fourth-hand, for years. For his birthday, friends—with the help of a Berlin bank—presented him with a new boat. It was a large sailboat with a mahogany deck, a galley, and sleeping space for four. Although Einstein was delighted with it, he was also overwhelmed. "Such magnificence," he said. "Why should I have this elaborate a boat?" But he loved the boat and sailed her whenever he could.

The city of Berlin surpassed even that gift. They gave Einstein a country home on the bank of the Havel River, near where it enters the Wannsee. But when Elsa went to inspect the house to see when they could move in, they found people living in it. The city of Berlin, it seemed, had agreed when it bought the land that the people living in the house could stay on there. The city council was much embarrassed. "All right," they agreed, "we will build another house for Einstein on the land." It turned out that that, too, was impossible. The people who had sold the land to the city had been guaranteed that no other house would ever be built. More embarrassed than ever, the council asked Einstein to pick out his own land. They would buy it for him. Einstein agreed, but let Elsa do the looking. After much searching, she found the perfect spot—in Caputh, a small town near Potsdam.

But when the subject came up in the next council meeting, debate began again. Perhaps the city had been too hasty, suggested some. Would Berlin now have to purchase a country home for all the physicists at the university? The intended gift became the subject of a heated political argument.

Finally Einstein lost patience. He had not expected the gift in the first place. If he did not have it, he would have lost very little. He wrote to the mayor of Berlin, declining the gift. Life, he felt, was much too short for him to waste time by becoming involved in this sort of petty political argument. The situation had, in fact, begun to distract him from his own important work.

Elsa was upset. The land had been so lovely and they had wanted a summer home for so long. Finally they bought the land themselves and built a low house of wood, with many windows. Elsa had a wonderful time furnishing it and it was to prove a retreat in the dread days ahead.

For Einstein, however, the most important event of his fiftieth year was the first publication of his Unified Field Theory. In his Special Theory of Relativity, he had treated only those bodies moving at uniform velocities. In the General Theory of Relativity, he had treated bodies moving at velocities that were not uniform. He had also proposed that space is curved, due to the force of gravity. He stated that this "force of gravity" was actually a gravitational field surrounding a body, somewhat analogous to the electromagnetic field surrounding an electric charge.

Ever since he had published his General Theory, Einstein had been trying to find a single theory which would account for both gravitational and electromagnetic fields. In developing this Unified Field Theory, he again worked with the concepts of four-dimensional space. (These concepts had made him realize the curvature of space when he worked on the General Theory.) Now at last he was ready to release his material. He sent the paper to the Prussian Academy of Science for publication.

When Einstein had originally published his first work on the Special Theory, he had expected physicists to be interested in what he was proposing. But he had not foreseen how great the interest would become. When he published his work on the General Theory, he again had expected to interest mainly the physicists. To his amazement and consternation, the general public became intensely interested. Articles appeared in all the papers and readers wrote letters to editors, upholding or denouncing Einstein's views. He knew that this interest in the General Theory made people listen to him when he spoke about peace and war, about Zionism and prejudice, but he had never been happy with all the attention. And then the news about his Unified Field Theory leaked out!

Reporters lay in wait for Einstein, outside his home and outside his office. Photographers followed him everywhere. Newspapers and magazines vied for the privilege of publishing the first stories about this theory. Some even tried bribing the printer used by the Prussian Academy, hoping for a look at the paper before the magazine was printed. Finally the material was published, and a copy of Einstein's short paper was telegraphed to New York, word by word.

Although the public was much interested in the theory, it was again only the scientists who understood it and appreciated its elegance. (In science, a theory is considered "elegant" if it explains a number of facts in the simplest manner possible.) Einstein showed in this first paper that the Unified Field Theory was a natural consequence of certain assumptions he had previously made about the nature of four-dimensional space. He was able to show, using abstract geometry, that both electromagnetic and gravitational fields were, indeed, special cases of the Unified Field Theory.

My abhorrence of militarism and war is as great as yours. Until about 1933 I advocated conscientious objection. But with the rise of Fascism I recognized that one could not maintain such a point of view except at the risk of allowing the whole world to fall into the hands of the most terrible enemies of mankind. Organized power can be opposed only by organized power. Much as I regret this, there is no other way.

Albert Einstein, from *Einstein on Peace*

# The Militant Pacifist

During the rest of 1929 and most of 1930, Albert Einstein continued to work for what he considered a necessity—a world at peace. Although at times almost despairing of the atmosphere in Germany, he continued to be the German representative to the Committee on Intellectual Cooperation. He continued, however, to have misgivings about the effectiveness and independence of the committee.

In 1930, Professor R. A. Millikan of the California Institute of Technology invited Einstein to become a visiting professor at CIT. Einstein accepted, and on November 30 he and his wife sailed for New York. Einstein rested and worked on the trip, but was uneasy over the reception he might get in America. He had not been in America for ten years. Would the reporters descend on him again, or would he be left alone as he wished? His worst fears were realized as hordes of reporters and photographers came aboard the ship before it docked. He answered the "inane questions" of the reporters as well as he could, then broadcast a message to the American people.

For the next five days, the Einsteins lived on a merry-go-round. There were press conferences, speeches to be made—

and listened to—sight-seeing trips, and formal ceremonies. Mayor James J. Walker gave him the keys to the city. He was taken to see the sculptured doors of Riverside Church, on which his head appears with that of other great philosophers. He met conductor Arturo Toscanini and the great violinist, Fritz Kreisler, as well as the Indian poet-philosopher Rabindranath Tagore. But late every night, the Einsteins were able to escape back to the ship, where guards protected their privacy. Einstein was much relieved when the ship sailed on its way to the West Coast through the Panama Canal. Einstein enjoyed his stay in Pasadena. He met and talked with some of America's outstanding physicists and astrophysicists who were at Mount Wilson Observatory. He toured Hollywood, and attended a private screening of *All Quiet on the Western Front*, which had been banned in Germany. In March of 1931 he returned to Berlin.

He had no sooner returned to Berlin than he plunged once again into politics. Emil J. Gumbel, a professor of philosophy at Heidelberg, Germany had been an active pacifist for many years. The reactionaries sought to discredit him, and had managed to get the department of philosophy at Heidelberg to censure him in 1925. Although due for a promotion, he never received it from the university. The government had finally, in 1931, given him a minor promotion. But many of the nationalist students and faculty members protested violently. Einstein came to Gumbel's defense, writing (in part), "We are assembled today to take stock of ourselves. The occasion for our meeting is the case of Professor Gumbel.

Inspired by an uncompromising sense of justice, Professor Gumbel publicized the details about a number of political crimes that have gone unavenged. He did so with devoted industry, high courage and exemplary fairness, performing through his books a signal service to our community. Yet this is the man whom the student body and a good many faculty members of his university are doing their best to expel." *cop. 8*

All through 1931, Einstein continued his efforts against war, at the same time continuing his scientific work. During May, he went to Oxford, England, where he delivered the Rhodes lectures. His topic was, "The Theory of Relativity: Its Formal Content and Its Present Problems." He was awarded still another honorary degree, yet found the time during that month to meet with pacifist students and with members of the War Resisters' International to discuss resistance to military conscription—today called the "draft."

During the early winter of 1931, Einstein went back to Pasadena. This time he avoided New York, taking a smaller ship that went directly to the West Coast. Pasadena was lovely in the winter, although Einstein noted that almost ten per cent of the people in Pasadena were unemployed, and that President Hoover was unwilling to do anything to cure this. He found time for many speeches on behalf of the pacifist movement while he was in California. He also wrote an article for the *Crisis*, the publication of the NAACP (National Association for the Advancement of Colored People), in which he stated:

"It seems to be a universal fact that minorities, especially

SISKIYOU COUNTY FREE LIBRARY
YREKA, CALIF.

when their individuals are recognizable because of physical differences, are treated by the majorities among whom they live as inferiors. The tragic part of such a fate, however, lies not only in the automatically realized disadvantages suffered by these minorities in economic and social relations, but also in the fact that those who meet such treatment themselves for the most part acquiesce in this prejudiced estimate because of the suggestible influence of the majority, and come to regard people like themselves as inferior.

"This second and more important aspect of the evil can be met through closer union and conscious educational enlightenment among the minority, and so an emancipation of the soul of the minority may be attained. The determined effort of the American Negroes in this direction deserves every recognition and assistance."

In March, the Einsteins sailed back to Germany, a Germany that had become increasingly bitter and torn by struggle between reactionaries and moderates. The March, 1932, presidential election in Germany was a fateful one. Field Marshal von Hindenburg was elected to the presidency, rather than Adolf Hitler. Most people the world over heaved a sigh of relief. The reactionary Hitler had been defeated—now politics would certainly settle down. In May, Einstein went to Geneva to attend the Disarmament Conference of the Joint Peace Council of the International Union of Antimilitarist Ministers and Clergymen. Einstein was merely an observer, not a delegate of any of the participating countries, yet his influence was great and his mere presence at the conference made many people feel that lasting progress might be made toward peace.

The Einsteins spent that summer in their beloved summer home at Caputh. Both of Elsa's daughters were married by this time, but they often came to visit with their husbands. Another visitor was Abraham Flexner, an American educator. He had conceived the idea of founding an Institute for Advanced Study at which leading mathematicians and scientists could work, consulting each other freely.

"The Institute will be at Princeton," he reminded Einstein. "We feel it will be incomplete without you on the staff. Come stay with us for part of the year at least."

"My home is here in Germany. How can I desert it now? Besides, I have already agreed to go back to Pasadena this winter—and I must go to Leyden, also, to lecture and to see my friends, the Kings."

"The Kings? I don't think I know them. Is Mr. King a physicist?"

"A physicist?" Einstein was astonished. "Why no, he is the king—of Belgium, you know. The Queen is a fine musician. She often plays second violin in our chamber music concerts when I am in Belgium. Yes, I owe the Kings a visit. So I cannot come to your new Institute, Flexner, although I like the idea very much."

"Perhaps next year, then."

"Next year might be different. If you really want me to come to Princeton, then I will tell Millikan I cannot come back to Pasadena."

"That's settled then." Flexner was relieved. He felt that he might as well get all the details settled at once. "What sort of tools would you need?"

"A pad of paper and a pencil. And a big wastepaper basket for all my mistakes. And perhaps a blackboard and some chalk —so I could write down some of my work for any visitor."

"That's easily gotten. We might even be able to stretch the budget for a blackboard eraser—for those mistakes you talk about. But how about salary? What would you like us to pay you?"

"Pay?" Einstein considered for a moment. "Would $6000 be all right?" Noting Flexner's startled look, Einstein went on humbly, "If not, I could get along with less."

Flexner laughed. "You are a wonderful man, Professor Einstein. But I don't think that $6000 is 'all right.' It is far too little. Would you object if Mrs. Einstein and I discussed this matter? I am sure we can agree on a figure."

"I would like it very much. Elsa has a much better head for figures than I. I never really know how much anything costs. She always scolds me about it, but you know, I think she secretly likes it this way."

The Institute of Intellectual Cooperation (sponsored by the committee on which Einstein had been a member) suggested to Einstein that he invite someone to exchange views on an important problem. Einstein was occupied as always with the problem of peace and war. Accordingly, he wrote to Sigmund Freud, inviting him to a public debate on the causes of war. The letters they interchanged in the summer of 1932 were

114

published in 1933 in a small pamphlet called *Why War?* In keeping with his feelings up to this time, Einstein felt that a supranational organization—able to make decisions on the international scene and to *enforce* them—had to be set up. (One of the failings of the League of Nations, obvious to everyone by 1933, was that it could not enforce its recommendations.) He went on to say: "Thus I am led to my first axiom: The quest of international security involves the unconditional surrender by every nation, in a certain measure, of its liberty of action—its sovereignty that is to say—and it is clear beyond all doubt that no other road can lead to such security."

Einstein developed this idea further and then went on to pose two important questions to Freud: "How is it that these devices succeed so well in rousing men to such wild enthusiasm, even to sacrifice their lives? Only one answer is possible. Because man has within him a lust for hatred and destruction. In normal times this passion exists in a latent state, it emerges only in unusual circumstances; but it is a comparatively easy task to call it into play and raise it to the power of a collective psychosis. Here lies, perhaps, the crux of all the complex factors we are considering, an enigma that only the expert in the lore of human instincts can resolve.

"And so we come to our last question. Is it possible to control man's mental evolution so as to make him proof against the psychosis of hate and destructiveness? Here I am thinking by no means only of the so-called uncultured masses. Experience proves that it is rather the so-called 'intelligensia' that is

115

most apt to yield to these disastrous collective suggestions, since the intellectual has no direct contact with life in the raw but encounters it in its easiest, synthetic form—upon the printed page."

Freud was delighted at this chance to exchange viewpoints with Einstein, particularly on such an important subject. He answered with a long, detailed letter in September of 1932. He agreed with Einstein's observations and went on to extend them into observations on the development of both violence and right (laws) from primitive societies, saying: "So far I have set out what seems to me the kernel of the matter: the suppression of brute force by the transfer of power to a larger combination, founded on the community of sentiment linking up its members . . . Now the position is simple enough so long as the community consists of a number of equipollent individuals. The laws of such a group can determine to what extent the individual must forfeit his personal freedom, the right of using personal force as an instrument of violence, to insure the safety of the group. But such a combination is only theoretically possible; in practice the situation is always complicated by the fact that, from the outset, the group includes elements of unequal power, men and women, elders and children, and, very soon, as a result of war and conquest, victors and the vanquished—i.e., masters and slaves—as well. From this time on the common law takes notice of these inequalities of power, laws are made by and for the rulers giving the servile classes fewer rights. Thenceforward there exist within the state two factors making for legal instability, but legislative evolution, too: first, the attempts by members of the ruling class to set themselves above the law's restrictions and, secondly, the constant struggle of the ruled to extend their rights and see each gain embodied in the code, replacing legal disabilities by equal laws for all."

Freud went on to agree with Einstein that there indeed was an instinct for hate and destruction (the death instinct) within everyone. Yet he also felt that there was an instinct for peace that perhaps could be used, although not in the near future. He felt that as human society became more "civilized," men would learn to overcome the destructiveness within them, even venturing the guess that ". . . if our ethical and aesthetic ideals have undergone a change, the causes of this are ultimately organic." He went on to say: "How long have we to wait before the rest of men turn pacifist? Impossible to say. . . ." Freud ended his letter on this hopeful note: "Meanwhile we may rest on the assurance that whatever makes for cultural development is working also against war."

Einstein was pleased with the response Freud had made and thanked him. Unfortunately, only about 2000 copies of the original German edition of the pamphlet were ever printed, and about the same number of the English version. Because of the rise of Hitler, very few people ever read these letters, and they thus had no discernible effect on the development of the coming war in Europe.

Because of his sponsorship of many peace organizations, Einstein became the target of much hatred. Many of these attacks came, unfortunately, from American women who identified themselves as "patriotic." Somewhat annoyed by one of these attacks, Einstein retorted: "In my opinion, the patriotic women ought to be sent to the front in the next war instead of the men. It would at least be a novelty in this dreary sphere of infinite confusion. And besides, why should not such heroic feelings on the part of the fair sex find a more picturesque outlet than in attacks on a defenseless civilian?"

Another group, learning that Einstein had made plans to come back to the United States for the winter of 1932-33, protested to the State Department that a visa should not be granted to such a person, since, they claimed, his membership in the War Resisters' International proved he was a Communist. Einstein promptly replied: "Never yet have I experienced from the fair sex such energetic rejection of all advances; or if I have, never from so many at once.

"But are they not right, these watchful citizenesses? Why should one open one's doors to a person who devours hard-boiled capitalists with as much appetite and gusto as the Cretan Minotaur in days gone by devoured luscious Greek maidens, and on top of that is low-down enough to reject every sort of war, except the unavoidable war with one's own wife? Therefore give heed to your clever and patriotic womenfolk and remember that the Capitol of mighty Rome was once saved by the cackling of its faithful geese."

The State Department rejected the appeal of this particular group of women.

Thus it was that the Einsteins were in Pasadena on January 30, 1933, when President von Hindenburg swore in Adolf

Hitler as Chancellor of Germany. Einstein was shocked. Although he knew that the reactionaries were becoming stronger in Germany, Einstein had never believed that they would be strong enough to form a government. Even the fact that new elections were promised on March 5 did not console him.

"You'll see," he predicted gloomily. The German people have always wanted a strong leader. This election will not change anything."

And then, on February 27, the Reichstag (the German parliamentary building) was set afire. Although a half-witted German Communist was eventually executed for the deed, most people inside and outside Germany suspected that he was only a dupe and that the Nazi party had set the fire for its own ends. For on the next day, February 28, Hitler persuaded the aged Hindenburg to sign a decree "For the Protection of the People and the State." This decree suspended the seven sections of the German constitution which guaranteed civil liberties to all German citizens. It was the beginning of the most brutal regime that the modern world has ever seen—a rule that lasted for twelve years and that took the combined forces of half the world to defeat.

Einstein was torn by indecision. Scientists and laymen alike looked to him for leadership. Where was his duty? Should he stay away from Germany or should he go back, hoping to aid the cause of reason before the coming election? But every day the news from Berlin became worse! The day of reason was over, and terror stalked the streets of Germany. Every day the denunciations of the German press against Communists and Jews became more and more hysterical. The press used the terms interchangeably, so that to accuse a person of being Jewish also at once accused him of being a Communist. Reporters again began begging Einstein for a story. Was he going back to Berlin as he had planned? Would he stay in America? Was he, perhaps, going to Belgium? Einstein could only reply that he had not yet been able to decide.

But by March 10, he had made his decision. Evelyn Seeley, of the New York World-Telegram, interviewed him. "I am not going home," he told her sadly, then went on, in words that have become famous: "As long as I have any choice in the matter, I shall live only in a country where civil liberty, tolerance, and equality of all citizens before the law prevail. Civil liberty implies freedom to express one's political convictions, in speech and in writing; tolerance implies respect for the convictions of others whatever they may be. These conditions do not exist in Germany at the present time. Men, among them leading artists, who have made a particularly great contribution to the cause of international understanding, are being persecuted there."

When Evelyn Seeley asked whether the Einsteins would stay in the United States, Einstein replied that they were going back to Europe, for a while at least. Perhaps to Switzerland, for Einstein had never relinquished his Swiss citizenship, although he had become a German citizen.

Although Einstein was welcomed warmly in New York, he and Elsa were impatient to get back to Europe. Their families were there, as well as their books, furniture, and other property. They sailed for Antwerp on March 17.

On March 20 came news that they had been expecting, yet dreading. The Nazis had raided the Einstein summer home near Caputh, stating that they were looking for an arms cache that had been hidden there. Although no arms had been found, Einstein's beloved sailboat was confiscated. This was followed shortly by the confiscation of all his property on the grounds that "this property was obviously going to be used to finance a Communist revolt."

The Einsteins went to the Belgian seaside resort of Le Cocque sur Mer. Here they waited for news of Ilse and Margot, who had left Berlin. Margot and her husband went directly to Paris; Ilse and her husband, to the Netherlands. Walter Mayer, Einstein's assistant, was now at the villa, as was Einstein's secretary, Helen Dukas.

But even with the enlarged household, Elsa could not rest easily. Le Cocque was too near the German border. It would be easy for an assassin to get across the border. The "Kings" worried about the safety of their famous friend, and guards were finally assigned to the villa.

Before going back to Europe, Einstein had canceled a projected lecture at the Prussian Academy of Science. Now he wrote to the Academy, reaffirming that he intended to renounce his Prussian citizenship and his membership in the Academy. Einstein, however, protested against the Academy's statement that he was atrocity-mongering in both America and France. The Academy accepted his resignation, but suggested that it was just as well that he had resigned, since he obviously was not going to defend the German people from attacks by their enemies. Einstein retorted that this suggestion by the Academy merely confirmed that he had been right to resign. He also resigned from the Bavarian Academy of Science, which had written asking him his intentions.

One by one, Einstein's ties to intellectuals in Germany were cut. Perhaps the hardest fact for him to accept was the manner in which his old friend Planck accepted his resignation. Rather than denouncing the Prussian Academy, as Einstein would have done had the situation been reversed, Planck felt that Einstein had spared his friends "immeasurable grief" by resigning when he did.

The Nazi repressions went on. Books were burned in Berlin's Opera Square at midnight on May 10. Students helped the storm troopers throw on the fire books by Freud, Mass, Remarque, Rathenau, and Einstein. The government barred Jews from the universities. Jewish doctors and lawyers could no longer practice. Thousands fled the country. But, surprisingly, many Jews in Germany, as well as in the rest of the world, felt that once the initial fury was spent the Nazis would leave them alone. They reasoned that if the Jews did nothing to provoke future attacks they would be safe—forgetting that the Jews had done nothing to provoke the initial attack.

Albert Einstein had spoken up frequently before for Zionism and for Jewish charities. Now he spoke and wrote against the Nazi government in Germany. To his horror, many Jews turned on him, accusing him of provoking the official anti-Semitism. Rabbi Stephen S. Wise of New York, himself under attack by Jewish groups, wrote to Einstein telling him of these attacks. Einstein replied that the conscience of the world, particularly America, had to be aroused. He felt that this might have some effect on Germany, although he conceded the possibility that the government might become more hostile if Jews in other lands protested.

That year he visited Oxford again, meeting Winston Churchill for the first time. Although Einstein still described himself as a pacifist, he was beginning to feel that military strength might be the only answer. In June he had been asked to appear in behalf of two conscientious objectors who were to be tried in Brussels. Einstein now had to make a decision. Was service in the armed forces of any country to be defended? Was it never right to intervene in a fight? Einstein wrestled with the questions, putting off the day of final reckoning.

Then, early in July, he received a letter from a lady-in-waiting to his friend, Queen Elizabeth of Belgium. This letter mentioned that "the husband of the second fiddler would like to see you on an urgent matter." Even in those grim days, a reference to the Queen's playing could draw a smile from Einstein. He now made up his mind quickly and was able to tell his friend, King Albert, and to reaffirm his decision in a letter, that he would not interfere in the case of the two young men. Abandoning a life-long belief, Einstein felt that in the threatening environment created by Germany, Belgium had a right and an obligation to defend herself. He wrote a second letter to the pacifist who had urged him to intervene: "Were

I a Belgian, I should not, in the present circumstances, refuse military service; rather, I should enter into such service cheerfully in the belief that I would thereby be helping to save European civilization."

Outraged pacifists now wrote to Einstein, denouncing him, demanding that he retract his statement. He was called an apostate and accused of going over to the military. But just as Einstein had been steadfast in his previous objections to military service, he was steadfast now. He was amazed that anyone should feel that he had deserted the cause of peace. He had simply become convinced that the way to serve peace was to see that France and Belgium could defend themselves against a probable German invasion. But the pacifists were not to be appeased. Attacks on Einstein continued.

The days of that grim summer went by, one by one. Each day brought news of some new horror. On August 31, Nazi agents killed Professor Theodor Lessing, a friend of Einstein's, who had fled to Czechoslovakia for safety. It appeared that there was no safety anywhere on the European continent. Einstein's family and friends felt he might be next. He was persuaded to go to England, where he stayed for more than a month in a small cabin on property owned by an English friend. Here, in the quiet and solitude that he craved but had not been granted for years, Einstein started to work again.

On October 3, 1933, Einstein made his final public appearance in England. The Refugee Assistance Fund, organized to aid scholars who had been exiled from Germany, was promoting a mass meeting at the Royal Albert Hall. The hall was heavily guarded, for Scotland Yard had learned that Einstein might be assassinated that night. Many people did not expect him to come. The audience of 10,000 waited tensely. Other leading figures in science were to speak that night, but everyone waited for Einstein. When Einstein finally came on stage, the crowd rose and gave him a standing ovation. His shy smile flashed briefly. Here at least, he felt, everyone was his friend.

He told the crowd how happy he was to address them, reminding them that he was not only a man, but a good European and a Jew. He felt that the two most important questions for the world were: "How could mankind and its cultural history be saved," and, "How could Europe be guarded from further disaster?" He went on:

"We are concerned not only with the technical problems of securing and maintaining peace but also with the important task of enlightenment and education. If we are to resist the powers that threaten intellectual and individual freedom, we must be very conscious of the fact that freedom itself is at stake; we must realize how much we owe to that freedom which our forefathers won through bitter struggle."

On October 17, 1933, the Einsteins, Walter Mayer, and Helen Dukas arrived in Princeton. Their new home at 112 Mercer Street would soon be ready for them. Einstein began going to his office, Room 209 in Fine Hall (the mathematics building) of Princeton. Eventually the Institute for Advanced Study built a new building, but at the start everyone had offices in Fine Hall. Residents of the community grew used to seeing Einstein walk quietly down the street.

Elsa's older daughter, Ilse, had not looked well when they left Europe. She had laughed at their fears, insisting that she was just tired. But when she visited Margot in Paris, Margot was shocked at her appearance.

"You look so tired and ill," Margot told her sister. "Why didn't you let us know? I would have come to see you rather than your making this trip."

Ilse protested faintly that she would be all right as soon as she rested a bit. But suddenly she became worse, and Margot cabled to her mother to come immediately. Elsa sailed at once, but things were as bad as they had feared. Ilse died shortly after her mother's arrival.

When Elsa came back, she looked like another woman. "It is a hard thing to bury your child," she told Albert. "The pain in my heart has never stopped. Perhaps it never will." Albert did his best to cheer her up, but she was never quite the same after this blow.

Albert was relieved when Margot came from Paris to stay with them. She was trying a trial separation from her husand, Dmitri Marianoff, who claimed that he could no longer support her. Although Margot's presence cheered her mother up somewhat, Margot herself was not happy at the time. Einstein was often glad to escape from the gloom of the house to his office in Fine Hall.

He was still working on a new formulation of his Unified Field Theory with Walter Mayer. Mayer, himself an accomplished mathematician, wanted to go on and do some of his

126

own work, not merely calculations for Einstein. When Mayer accepted an independent job at the Institute for Advanced Study, Einstein was forced to look around for someone else to assist him. There were many people who wished to work with Einstein, but he felt that most of them lacked both originality and persistence. Young German scientists found their way to Princeton. Einstein usually arranged for them to work with someone else. Finally, Nathan Rosen, who had recently received his Ph.D. from Massachusetts Institute of Technology, became his assistant. They worked well together, and once more Einstein began publishing papers.

During the next year, the Einsteins decided to apply for American citizenship. Since they had originally arrived on visitor's visas, they had to reapply for emigration visas. In May of 1935, therefore, Einstein and Elsa, Margot and Helen Dukas went to Bermuda to apply for permanent visas. When they came back, summer had arrived in Princeton. That year they decided to spend the summer at Old Lyme, Connecticut. They rented a large house with both a tennis court and a swimming pool. But for Einstein, the summer was complete because he was able to have a sailboat again. He spent the long summer days on board ship, sailing and thinking, often writing letters to people active in aiding refugees from Nazi Germany.

Elsa had not been well all summer. They returned to Princeton, but even home did not make her feel better. She tired more and more easily and Einstein became more and more concerned. The burden of running the household fell on

Margot. Margot had finally divorced her husband and welcomed any opportunity to stay busy so she did not need to think about the future.

The winter passed slowly, and in the spring Elsa showed a slight improvement. That summer they spent quietly in Princeton, Einstein walking to work every day as usual.

In the early fall, Einstein had a young visitor. For a minute he did not recognize the man—then he knew him, Leopold Infeld. Einstein had helped Infeld gain admittance to the University of Berlin some years before. Now here he was in Einstein's Princeton office.

"But this is wonderful, my dear Infeld," Einstein said. "You came just at the right time. I have been puzzling over something. Perhaps you can help. Come over to the blackboard and let me show you."

Infeld studied the equations, then made a few suggestions. Einstein was delighted. Would Infeld like to work with him at the Institute? Good, that was settled then. And why didn't Infeld come home for dinner? And perhaps he should notify someone that Infeld had agreed to work with him? That way Infeld could get a fellowship. Infeld agreed to all this readily. Einstein looked older and more careworn, but his thoughts still raced ahead.

By this time, Elsa was very ill. She refused to go to a hospital, though, feeling that she would miss her home and family too much. Einstein shook his head despairingly.

"Very well, then. I will bring the hospital to you. We will get a nurse to look after you. And I will work at home. That way I can be here whenever you want me."

By the beginning of December, it was evident that Elsa was dying. Einstein spent long periods at her bedside, talking with her and reading to her. Even when she became too weak to talk, it comforted her to open her eyes and see him. On December 21, 1936, Elsa Einstein died. Now there was no refuge for Einstein except his work.

Soon after Elsa died, Hans Albert came to the United States to visit his father. But where was the joking father he remembered? This quiet, worn man—how his father had changed! Hans Albert stayed in Princeton for a month, then left for a tour of the United States. He came back with good news.

"I have decided to stay here," he told his father and Margot. "I have been offered a job as a soil chemist with the Agricultural Department in South Carolina. It is just what I have wanted to do, and this way I can see you more often. And perhaps it is time for you to see your grandchildren more often also." Einstein was pleased, although he would never have urged the young man to make this decision.

Meantime, Einstein and Infeld collaborated on a book, *The Evolution of Physics*. Although they had started the work to aid Infeld after his fellowship ran out, both men were surprised when it hit the best-seller list after its publication in 1938. After the first book, Infeld wrote a biography of Einstein, *The Quest*. Infeld left Princeton to go to the University of Toronto. After that, Einstein worked with Peter G. Bergmann and Vallentin Bargmann.

129

Now that we have the atomic secret, we must not lose it, and this is what we would risk doing if we gave it to the United Nations Organization or to the Soviet Union. But, as soon as possible, we must make it clear that we are not keeping the bomb a secret for the sake of maintaining our power but in the hope of establishing peace through world government, and that we will do our utmost to bring this world government into being.

Albert Einstein, from *Einstein on Peace*

# War and Postwar Years

Einstein kept on with the work he had decided on doing so many years ago. He knew that he was no longer in the mainstream of physics, but he felt that eventually others would come back to his views. Niels Bohr, the Danish physicist, was one of those who felt strongly about differing with Einstein. Now he was on his way to a scientific meeting in America and would later spend time with Einstein working out their differences. But when he landed in New York, he received a cablegram from Lise Meitner in Copenhagen. The cable read simply, "Success." Lise Meitner, the half-Jewish physicist who had fled Nazi Germany, had gone on with the work that she and Otto Hahn had started. She had now proved that uranium fission was possible and that Einstein's original $E = mc^2$ held true. The component pieces weighed less than the original mass; the difference had been released as energy.

Bohr announced this fact at the meeting in Washington in January, 1939. Scientists immediately started duplicating the experiments successfully. There was no longer any doubt. Atomic fission was a reality. Within a year, more than 100 papers would be published on this topic. Among the workers were Enrico Fermi, Leo Szilard, and Walter H. Zinn. They thought that it might be possible to start a chain reaction, using uranium as fuel. Although the Navy at first was interested, it later decided that it could not support this work. Meanwhile, Hitler had seized Czechoslovakia and Sir Neville Chamberlain had gone to Munich and returned with, as he put it, "peace in our time."

Szilard and Wigner were much disturbed by the knowledge that fine physicists in Germany were working on this problem. Suppose, they thought, the Germans are successful? They knew that there were rich deposits of uranium in the Belgian Congo and feared that Germany would insist on Belgium selling this raw material. Szilard knew of Einstein's friendship with Queen Elizabeth of Belgium, so he proposed that they ask Einstein to write to her and tell her what the situation was.

On July 15, 1939, Szilard and Wigner visited Einstein at Nassau Point, Long Island, where he was spending the summer. They convinced him of the possibility of a chain reaction, causing Einstein to exclaim: *"Daran habe ich nicht gedacht!"* (I never thought about that!) Of course he would write to Queen Elizabeth. They also agreed that the State Department would have to approve such a letter. Szilard returned to New York to draft the letter.

Once back in New York, Szilard contacted Dr. Alexander Sachs, an investment banker, who was one of President Roosevelt's advisers. Dr. Sachs felt the matter should be brought to the President's attention, rather than to that of the Belgian Queen. He offered to see that the letter got to the President, if Einstein wished. Szilard was impressed by Sachs and notified Einstein that they should take his advice. Szilard and Edward Teller then visited Einstein again, and Einstein agreed to the plan. He dictated a German draft to Teller. Szilard took this draft and prepared two English versions of it. Einstein liked the shorter version, and on August 2, 1939, Einstein signed the famous letter. This letter began:

"Some recent work by E. Fermi and L. Szilard, which has been communicated to me in manuscript, leads me to expect that the element uranium may be turned into a new and important source of energy in the immediate future. Certain aspects of the situation seem to call for watchfulness and, if necessary, quick action on the part of the administration. I believe, therefore, that it is my duty to bring to your attention the following facts and recommendations. . . ."

This letter was not delivered by Sachs to Roosevelt until early October. By that time, Europe had gone to war, ostensibly over Poland, but actually because everyone thought that a stand finally had to be taken against the Germans. Sachs convinced the President of the importance of Einstein's letter and the technical memorandum from Szilard. President Roosevelt responded by appointing an Advisory Committee on Uranium, composed of the head of the National Bureau of Standards and a representative from the Army Ordnance Department and from the Navy Bureau of Ordnance. The Manhattan project, Oak Ridge, and Los Alamos all followed in time.

Einstein's sister, Maja, had come to Princeton to stay with

him. Her husband, the same Karl Winteler whom Einstein had been so friendly with as a young man, stayed in Switzerland. Maja was unable to get back to Europe because of the war, and her presence was always comforting to Einstein. And in October, 1940, Einstein, Helen Dukas, and Margot took the oath of citizenship. Once more Einstein had a country.

Einstein had never done any war work. He did not propose to start now, at this time in life. Rather, he would try to go on with his own work in Fuld Hall, the new home of the Institute. He agreed to play his violin at a benefit concert arranged by the American Friends Service Committee, and he aided other charitable causes.

The war in Europe went on. The Japanese attacked the United States Fleet in Pearl Harbor on December 7, 1941. Now Einstein's new country was also at war. The Navy Bureau of Ordnance finally asked Einstein if he would do some work for them on the theory of explosions, to find out how the direction of an explosion is determined. Emphasizing that this work was strictly theoretical, the Bureau of Ordnance finally convinced Einstein. Now he, too, was involved in war work.

President Roosevelt ran for a fourth term. Einstein was among those who supported him, and he was among the millions who were stricken at Roosevelt's sudden death from a cerebral hemorrhage. On May 8, 1945, President Truman announced that the war in Europe was over. Einstein was grateful, although since the murder of six million Jews by the Nazis he had given up thinking about the Europe he had left.

But the war in the Pacific was still to be won.

Einstein formally retired from the Institute of Advanced Study in April, 1945, a month after he turned sixty-six. His daily routine did not change, however, and he continued to go to his office in Fuld Hall every day. During the summer the household moved to Saranac Lake, a beautiful resort in the evergreen forests of upper New York state. Einstein was there on the day the White House announced that the "Enola Gay" had made a successful flight run over Hiroshima, Japan. The first atomic bomb had been dropped and the course of the war changed. The world would never be the same! A second bomb was dropped on Nagasaki. The Japanese surrender came soon afterward and, for the first time since 1931 when the Japanese had originally invaded China, the guns were still.

The dropping of the bomb caused a great reaction among physicists. Although they had known they were working on the problem, they had never really expected the bomb to be dropped. Many scientists had thought that if enemy leaders were invited to see a demonstration of the bomb, the actual use of the bomb would be unnecessary. Einstein himself had signed the original letter to President Roosevelt because he had thought that the Germans might perfect such a bomb. He had not anticipated that the bomb would be used if Germany surrendered.

Certain scientists supported the decision to use the bomb. President Truman had made this decision on the basis that it would probably make the Japanese surrender more quickly.

Otherwise, he felt, a long invasion of Japan would have to be made, which would surely cost many lives, both American and Japanese. The destruction that even an ordinary bomb would have caused in most Japanese cities would be much greater than in Europe, since the buildings were primarily of wood and paper—and thus were highly inflammable. Better one or two atom bombs than hundreds of thousands of conventional bombs preceding an invasion.

The reaction of the scientists who were working on the atomic bomb was matched by the stunned horror of most of the public. When pictures of blast and radiation damage became widely circulated after the Japanese surrender, a wave of revulsion set in. Many, many people blamed the scientists for the bomb and felt that this *proved* that scientists and intellectuals could not be trusted. This feeling undoubtedly helped pave the way for the anti-intellectualism of the United States in the 1950's and the attacks made on freedom of conscience and academic freedom. It is an ironic fact that those people who attacked the scientists for their social irresponsibility would have been among the first to attack them during the war if the same scientists had refused to do weapons research.

During the postwar years Einstein's health was poor and he had to refuse most invitations to speak. Yet he believed strongly in the necessity of a supranational organization, such as the United Nations, with the power to enforce decisions made for the common good of all mankind. (He excepted only the Germans who had "slain my Jewish brothers.") He wrote extensively on this problem and was happy to serve as chairman of the Emergency Committee of Atomic Scientists.

Einstein continued to work for the establishment of the Jewish homeland and for aid for the pitiful remnants of European Jewry. Surely, he felt, the conscience of the world must wince at the sight—so few left, over six million slaughtered.

Einstein continued to express himself on civic and social issues. Prejudice had touched him; now safe in America he felt he had to speak out on those moral issues he saw. In 1946 he wrote:

"There is, however, a somber point in the social outlook of Americans. Their sense of equality and human dignity is mainly limited to men of white skins. Even among these there are prejudices of which I as a Jew am clearly conscious; but they are unimportant in comparison with the attitude of the "Whites" toward their fellow-citizens of darker complexion, particularly toward Negroes. The more I feel an American, the more this situation pains me. I can escape the feeling of complicity in it only by speaking out."

He ended: "What, however, can the man of good will do to combat this deeply rooted prejudice? He must have the courage to set an example by word and deed, and must watch lest his children become influenced by this racial bias.

"I do not believe there is a way in which this deeply entrenched evil can be quickly healed. But until this goal is reached, there is no greater satisfaction for a just and well-meaning person than the knowledge that he has devoted his best energies to the service of the good cause."

Time continued to bring unhappy changes. Maja Einstein became ill and finally bedridden in 1946. She could no longer accompany Albert on trips to Saranac, so he no longer went. Paul Langevin, the last of Einstein's European scientist friends, died in 1947. Now the last link with the world of European science had snapped. One by one they go, Einstein thought sadly; soon I will be the only one left.

The year 1948 continued the tragic tale. Mileva died in Zurich, where she had always remained. Shortly afterward, Maja died. Einstein felt more and more alone. Of all his friends, only Queen Elizabeth of Belgium was still alive. And Einstein himself was dangerously ill. He had been plagued by stomach pains for half his life; now the doctors felt he might have an intestinal cyst. He went into the Jewish Hospital in Brooklyn and Dr. Rudolf Nissen, also a German Jewish refugee, removed several cysts. Dr. Nissen also found that Einstein's liver was not functioning properly, but that could be helped by the proper medicine.

Family and friends insisted that Einstein convalesce in the warm climate of Florida. In all the years of fame, Einstein had never accepted the idea of luxury; it still made him uncomfortable. But, grumbling or not, off he went for a rest. When he returned to Princeton shortly before spring, he looked and felt considerably better than he had in a long time.

He went back to work with renewed vigor. He was still trying to find a way of showing that all types of fields created by different forces were special cases of one law. He felt that the same physical laws must apply to matter, whether in the world of the atomic nucleus or the world of the cosmos. He finally arrived at a new formulation of his Unified Field Theory, which was published late in 1949. However, other physicists still remained unconvinced.

Einstein's seventieth birthday had been on March 14, 1949. He had spent the day quietly with his friends. Some six months later the book that had originally been planned as a seventieth birthday gift came out. At the urging of Paul Arthur Schilpp, professor of philosophy at Northwestern University and editor of *Albert Einstein: Philosopher-Scientist*, Einstein had contributed some "Autobiographical Notes," the only autobiographical material he ever wrote. The list of contributors to the book reads like an honor roll of atomic scientists; Sommerfeld, de Broglie, Pauli, Born, Bohr, Bridgman—all the great minds of quantum physics joined in paying tribute to Albert Einstein's work and in reaffirming that he had shaped the course of physics by his pioneering papers of 1905 and later.

Einstein was touched by this appreciation, but he continued to work. In 1952, his old friend Chaim Weizmann died. Israel mourned her beloved president, and then offered the presidency to Albert Einstein. Much as he appreciated the honor, Einstein felt he could not accept. He knew he had little skill at handling people—the newspapers were always misinterpreting his statements. Besides, there was his work; that would suffer if he had to leave Princeton and go to Israel for what was mainly an honorary job. He regretfully declined.

He was still active in American politics, however, and was

one of the first people to denounce publicly Senator Joseph McCarthy. At a time when it seemed almost foolhardy to say anything about the man who was getting so much publicity for fighting "Communists" in governmental circles, Einstein spoke up. At the height of the red witch-hunt in the colleges and universities, Einstein spoke up for intellectual freedom and the right of everyone to make his own decisions.

Honors continued to come to him. He accepted most of them with wry humor, realizing that the world had long since lost sight of Einstein the man, and now saw only Einstein the symbol. Yeshiva University, a Jewish university in New York, asked for permission to name their new school of medicine after him. On his seventy-fourth birthday, he went to a fund-raising luncheon given by Yeshiva University in his honor. It was one of his last public appearances.

His seventy-fifth birthday he spent quietly with friends. He was still working, although more and more he worked at home, for the walk to Fuld Hall tired him too much. He regretfully declined an invitation to go to Switzerland as guest of honor at a scientific congress on the fiftieth anniversary of relativity.

Although he had had to decline the presidency, Israel was still close to his heart. He was asked whether he would make a speech on Israel's anniversary, and he himself suggested that he prepare "a critical analysis of the policies of the Western nations with regard to Israel and the Arab states . . ." On April 11, Israeli Ambassador Abba Eban and the Consul came to Princeton to see him. On April 13, the Consul came back to discuss Einstein's first draft with him. But the address was never completed. Two hours after the Consul left, Einstein became fatally ill. He was rushed to the hospital in Princeton, where he appeared to rally for a while.

"I still have lots of work to do," he reassured Hans Albert who had flown in from California. "I will get well again so I can finish my work." But on April 18, 1955, his stout heart finally gave out. The world mourned one of her scientific geniuses who was also one of the most humane of her sons.

# Acknowledgments

We are grateful to the Trustees of the Estate of Albert Einstein, particularly Dr. Otto Nathan, for having given permission to reproduce passages from *Einstein On Peace*, edited by Otto Nathan and Heinz Norden, and *Out of My Later Years*, by Albert Einstein.

Quotations from *Albert Einstein: Philosopher-Scientist*, edited by Paul Arthur Schilpp, were reprinted by arrangement with The Open Court Publishing Company (the present publishers of The Library of Living Philosophers) LaSalle, Illinois, and The Library of Living Philosophers, Inc.

Quotations from *Ideas and Opinions* by Albert Einstein, copyright 1954 by Crown Publishers, Inc., were used by permission of the publishers.

Quotations from an article appearing in the April, 1951 issue of the *Ladies Home Journal*, "Einstein Is My Father," told to Bela Kornitze by Hans Albert Einstein, were used by permission of the *Ladies Home Journal* and the Curtis Publishing Company.

# Suggested for Further Reading

Einstein, Albert. *Relativity, The Special and General Theory.* Crown Publishers, New York, 1961. (In paperback)

Einstein, Albert. *Ideas and Opinions.* Crown Publishers, New York, 1954.

Einstein, Albert. *Out of My Later Years.* Philosophical Library, New York, 1950.

Frank, Philipp. *Einstein: His Life and Times.* Alfred A. Knopf, New York, 1947.

Nathan, Otto and Norden, Heinz (eds.). *Einstein on Peace.* Simon and Schuster, New York, 1906.

Schilpp, Paul Arthur (ed.). *Albert Einstein: Philosopher-Scientist.* Library of Living Philosophers, 1949; 2nd ed. printed 1951.

Shirer, William L. *The Rise and Fall of the Third Reich.* Simon and Schuster, New York, 1960.

## *Credits*

Designer/BERT RAY STUDIO

Illustrations by/PARVIZ SADIGHIAN

Cover Painting/MARY GEHR

Type/CALEDONIA

Paper/ 70# PUBLISHERS OFFSET

Printer/REGENSTEINER CORPORATION

# Index